THE LAST YEARS OF STEAM
— AROUND —
THE EAST MIDLANDS

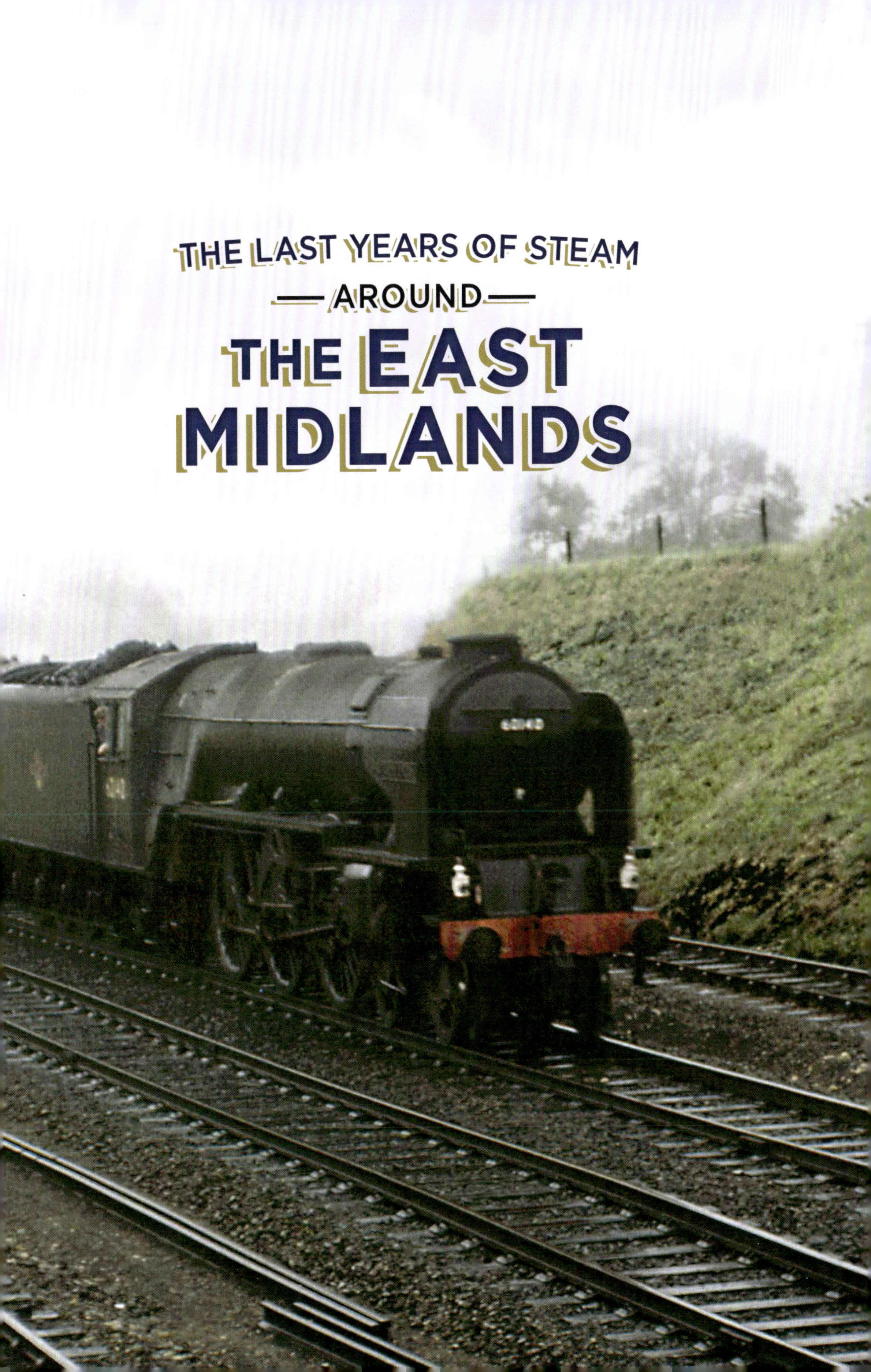

No. 46522 simmers away at Banbury engine shed on Thursday, 29 September 1966; this depot will close over the coming weekend and No. 46522 will find a new home at Carnforth.

The last day services called at Launton (between Bicester and Bletchley); an Oxford-bound DMU is about to depart on 30 December 1967.

THE LAST YEARS OF STEAM
—AROUND—
THE EAST MIDLANDS

MICHAEL CLEMENS

The entrance to Winslow Station on 30 December 1967; our family Ford Corsair (OAB 590E) looks rather grubby.

Fonthill Media Language Policy

Fonthill Media publishes in the international English language market. One language edition is published worldwide. As there are minor differences in spelling and presentation, especially with regard to American English and British English, a policy is necessary to define which form of English to use. The Fonthill Policy is to use the form of English native to the author. Michael Clemens was born and educated in Worcestershire, England; therefore British English has been adopted in this publication.

Fonthill Media Limited
Fonthill Media LLC
www.fonthillmedia.com
office@fonthillmedia.com

First published in the United Kingdom and the United States of America 2017

British Library Cataloguing in Publication Data:
A catalogue record for this book is available from the British Library

Copyright © Michael Clemens 2017

ISBN 978-1-78155-428-9

The right of Michael Clemens to be identified as the author of this work has been asserted by him in accordance with the Copyright, Designs and Patents Act 1988.

All rights reserved. No part of this publication may be reproduced, stored in a retrieval system or transmitted in any form or by any means, electronic, mechanical, photocopying, recording or otherwise, without prior permission in writing from Fonthill Media Limited

Typeset in 10.5pt on 13pt Sabon
Printed and bound by CPI Group (UK) Ltd, Croydon, CR0 4YY

Looking up the LNWR main line at Roade towards London Euston on a Sunday afternoon in October 1959.

Turvey station is seen just before the passenger service ceased in March 1962. This view is looking towards Northampton.

Part of a GWR map from the early twentieth century that covers much of the area visited in this book.

The signal is clear for No. 48065 at Desford Junction in March 1963; behind is Johnson 2F No. 58143, which will work the branch to Leicester, West Bridge.

No. 60022 *Mallard* holds the world record for a steam locomotive, which it achieved on Stoke Bank in 1938. This is *Mallard* in the rain, descending Stoke Bank in July 1962.

Introduction

My father (C. N. 'Jim' Clemens, 1922–1987) had a keen interest in railways. As a result, from a very early age, I often accompanied him from our Worcestershire home on visits around the country from Cornwall to the north of Scotland. He was fully aware by the 1950s that the railways of Britain were disappearing at an ever-increasing rate, plus the steam locomotives working over them were being scrapped, and he set out to record this vanishing scene. What I do not think he realised was the interest there would be in this subject fifty or more years later. Equally, I am sure it would have come as a surprise to him that the cine film we took at the time is the largest collection of its type in the UK, and over thirty videos of this movie film archive have been released since the 1990s. In recent times, I have concentrated on our collection of still photographs and this is my ninth photo-book about British railways and fifth for Fonthill Media.

The Last Years of Steam Around the East Midlands follows a similar format to my earlier books. It is the uniqueness of its photographs (both monochrome and colour) that will appeal to most as virtually all of the images have never been previously published. Most of the photographs were taken either by my late father or me (together with a handful by friends Paul Cowley and R. E. 'Ellis' James-Robertson) and all, with just a single exception, date from the 1950s or 1960s. The western boundary of this book is approximately the GWR main line from the West Midlands towards London; the eastern border broadly follows the East Coast Main Line from Newark to London King's Cross; while the northern edge is marked by Hatton, Nuneaton, Burton-on-Trent, and Nottingham. Despite the fact that there are photographs along the main lines, it is probably the secondary routes and branch lines that will be of interest to most. Also, the East Midlands still had numerous ironstone railways at the beginning of the 1960s and a number of these are included. Steam is the predominant motive power throughout, although there are diesel and electric examples, plus some DMUs; it will appeal to railway enthusiasts, modellers, and those interested in local history.

The main body of this book begins on a summer Saturday in 1962 as a holiday-maker service returning to the West Midlands from the South Coast climbs Hatton Bank. We then proceed to Fenny Compton, a junction station with the cross-country Stratford-upon-Avon and Midland Junction Railway that

Banbury during the summer of 1966 and No. 48766 is visiting from Stoke.

The LCGB 1 March 1959 tour of lines around Burton-on-Trent is seen at Woodville Goods.

Claydon, between Bicester and Bletchley, on the last day it was open: 30 December 1967.

will feature again in our travels across the East Midlands. Banbury General was a railway crossroads and saw regular steam-hauled express services until as late as September 1966. There also used to be another station at Banbury—Merton Street—and here from 1956 until the end of 1960, BR conducted an experiment on the Buckingham route to try and improve the economics of rural branch lines. Although the line from Bicester to Bletchley closed as a through passenger route from the beginning of 1968, it is due to be rebuilt as this book is being written, in order to recreate a direct link between Oxford and Cambridge. The line and its stations are seen bathed in a low winter sun just before closure.

On 1 August 1963, a journey is started from Nuneaton (where electrification work was underway) that largely follows the LNWR route towards London. On the way, visits are made to Daventry, Blisworth, Towcester, Roade, and Northampton. The Newport Pagnell branch is seen in 1962 and also in the summer of 1964, just before closure to passengers. A branch that made a lasting impression was that from Leighton Buzzard to Dunstable and Luton and, in particular, the intermediate station of Stanbridgeford. I was clearly not the only person who thought this station was decrepit and peculiar as it was used in an episode of *The Avengers* after closure. Four of the photographs along this branch were taken by Paul Cowley as a schoolboy, my wife Barbara and I met Paul and his wife Sue on a cruise to Spitsbergen, where we discovered a common interest in railways.

Bedford is approached over the Midland Railway line via Piddington and Olney, after which we move to ironstone country. Visits are made to both the Irchester and metre-gauge Finedon systems near Wellingborough, the Storefield pits near

The largest of the ironstone railway systems was at Corby, it boasted this impressive 1954-built engine shed where No. 35 stands outside in May 1965.

Evidence of your author (born August 1951) exploring the railways of the East Midlands at a very young age, seen here at Leicester West Bridge during August 1954.

Leighton Buzzard on 30 June 1962—the final service from Dunstable has arrived with No. 41222.

Kettering, and the biggest ironstone system of them all at Corby. In the late 1960s, surplus BR 'D95xx' diesel-hydraulics, built at Swindon only a few years earlier, were purchased for use at Corby, and we see the locomotive once numbered D9547 by BR. After visiting the Higham Ferrers branch, Irthlingborough, Cohen's scrapyard, Uppingham (in both 1954 and 1963), and Market Harborough, we arrive at Leicester and admire the city's Great Northern Railway terminus at Belgrave Road, as well as Humberstone and Ingarsby stations. One of England's first railways was the Leicester and Swannington that opened in 1832 to bring coal from the West Leicestershire coalfield—its arrival saw the price of coal almost halved in Leicester. Although passenger services had ceased at the line's Leicester West Bridge station in 1928, it was still open for freight, and, because of the restricted clearance through Glenfield Tunnel, this branch became the last haunt of Johnson's 2F 0-6-0s dating from the 1870s. By 1958, my father was using a Super Baldina 35-mm camera with Ilford FP3 film, a combination that produced excellent photographs, and the results can be seen at the LNWR station of Loughborough Derby Road in June 1958. There were a maze of branches and sidings around Burton-on-Trent serving the breweries and, on 1 March 1959, the LCGB organised a tour of this area, where again the Super Baldina and FP3 film combination was used.

Next, Newark North Gate in April 1961, to start a journey up the East Coast Main Line (ECML) to London King's Cross. The British summer weather was at its worst when a Saturday in 1962 was spent watching the activity on Stoke Bank,

No. 44847 waits for custom at Nottingham Victoria on 26 May 1966, hauling the evening service to London Marylebone.

With overhead electrification work underway, 'Jubilee' No. 45624 *St Helena* shunts at Nuneaton Trent Valley on 1 August 1963.

Looking south at Rugby Central in the evening sunshine of 16 June 1966, 'Black 5' No. 44835 is running round empty stock.

the place where the world speed record for a steam locomotive was achieved in 1938. Earlier, I said the eastern border for this book was the ECML; however, there are two main exceptions to this, and they both relate to the time my father was a Director of Worcester City Football Club. He would often attend away matches and fitted in visits to Sutton Bridge and South Lynn during the spring of 1960 while attending a match at King's Lynn—thanks to the King's Lynn FC website, I have been able to precisely date these visits to 23 March 1960 (Worcester City won). Peterborough is visited next before moving on to another of the ironstone sites at Nassington near Wansford, and then on to Huntingdon East. We had relatives at Welwyn Garden City and my father's first job was at the Murphy Radio factory there; he bicycled from Pershore, Worcestershire to Welwyn on the morning of Sunday 3 September 1939, and when he arrived, he found the country was at war. Photographs follow on the Hertford Loop, Hertford itself, and then Welwyn, before arrival at London King's Cross.

In broad terms, this book has followed the various main lines connecting to London that run across the East Midlands (GWR, LNWR, MR, and GNR) and we now travel along the very last of these built during the Victorian Era—the Great Central Railway northwards from London Marylebone. Being last on the railway map, the route suffered in that many of the places along its London extension were already served by other companies. With the growth of car ownership in the 1950s, plus the reduction in passengers travelling by rail, it became a prime

Woodford Halse looks rather derelict; it closed less than two months after this view of No. 45292 on 9 July 1966 awaiting departure for the north.

target for economy because of this duplication, and ended up as something of a secondary route. By 1966, the through-passenger service to Nottingham Victoria was just three semi-fasts during the day, with nothing on Sundays. We head north through Aylesbury, Quainton Road, Brackley, Helmdon for Sulgrave, and, after passing Culworth Junction, arrive at Woodford Halse. This was another place that had a junction with the east-to-west SMJR, and we visit Byfield plus its ironstone railway. Continuing north through Charwelton and its ironstone line, we then see the impressive Catesby Tunnel; who would have thought, fifty years ago, that today this tunnel would be being converted into a test track for high-speed motor cars? At Rugby, this book's only electric locomotives put in an appearance—Metropolitan Railway Bo-Bos awaiting the cutter's torch—before moving on through Lutterworth to Leicester. At Loughborough, the Brush works are passed, their yard full of brand new 'Type 4' diesels plus the largely forgotten experimental diesel locomotive *Hawk*. Our journey around the East Midlands concludes at Nottingham Victoria; this station's formal opening occurring on Queen Victoria's birthday in 1900. Building Nottingham Victoria was a massive undertaking, involving the removal of some 600,000 cubic yards of sandstone from a site about 650 yards long and 110 yards wide, and there was a tunnel at each end. Despite passenger services being run down in later years, it was still possible to appreciate the splendour of this much-missed station.

For those interested in further coverage of this area, I have released an eighty-minute-long video of the region—East Midland Railways—using cine film taken by my father and myself. Further details can be found on my website, which also includes hundreds of pages of freely downloadable archive railway material, such as all the tickets used throughout this book and original sound recordings associated with some of the photographs—michaelclemensrailways.co.uk.

I would like to thank, in no particular order, various societies and individuals who have freely given me their help in compiling this book: Severn Valley Railway Association (Stourbridge Branch); Shirley Railway Club; Cheltenham Railway Action Photographers; Chipping Norton Railway Society; Mark Ratcliffe of the Burton Railway Society; David Postle of the Kidderminster Railway Museum; Paul Cowley, for help with the proof reading of this book; and, finally, the late G. E. S. 'Eric' Parker of Worcester (1900–1988), whose diaries have been an invaluable source of information.

Michael Clemens
Pershore, Worcestershire
December 2016

Passenger services ceased at Sutton Bridge in 1959. This view dates from March 1960.

Cock o' the North, its double chimney prominent, passes through Welwyn North in the spring of 1958.

THE LAST YEARS OF STEAM
— AROUND —
THE EAST MIDLANDS

The last day of the push-pull service between Leighton Buzzard and Dunstable North was 30 June 1962. No. 41222 calls at Stanbridgeford.

The Last Years of Steam around the East Midlands commences following its western border, the GWR main line from Birmingham Snow Hill to London Paddington, and along which the principle expresses remained with steam until the end of the 1962 summer timetable. This is Hatton Bank to the west of Warwick, over 3 miles at a maximum grade of 1 in 103. The third track on the right allows slow and heavy freight trains to be kept separate from faster passenger services; it still exists today. On a summer Saturday in 1962, and taken on Perutz film, a through train from the South Coast to the West Midlands, composed of Southern Region green coaching stock, is making its way uphill. These holiday-maker services ran from destinations such as Portsmouth, Bournemouth, Margate, Eastbourne, and Hastings. In charge is one of the Churchward-designed 2-6-0s, first built over fifty years previously, although by

1962, the earliest examples had already been withdrawn. The class were a great success and could cope with goods work, yet also be fast and steady enough for passenger trains. They were a 'maid-of-all-work' of the era and well over 300 were built; Churchward said the type 'obviates the necessity of keeping so varied a stock of engines in the running sheds'. An advantage still being exploited in 1962 was their relatively light (17.6 tons) axle load, as it enabled the class to work right through from Redhill over the line to Reading, and then on to the West Midlands. Dark Lane road bridge achieved notoriety in November 1954 when part of its right-hand side collapsed; it was rebuilt, but the slight colour difference between the two sides is still visible nearly eight years later.

Above: Taken towards the end of the 1962 summer timetable, No. 6022 *King Edward III* is about to pass Fenny Compton in fading light with the 5.10 p.m. express from London Paddington to Birmingham Snow Hill and Wolverhampton Low Level. In 1959, it was decided to speed up electrification of the old LMS lines out of London Euston and, to allow engineers maximum time occupation of the West Coast Main Line, the service from Euston to Birmingham New Street and Wolverhampton High Level was reduced by five trains in each direction. There was a corresponding increase on the old GWR route through Fenny Compton from nine in each direction to fifteen down and fourteen up trains. Around two years previously, the service was operated by 'Kings' and 'Castles' in about equal proportions, but dieselisation of the West Country services beginning in 1958 released 'Kings' that could now be used on the enhanced West Midlands trains, and they now predominated. By early 1960, of the thirty 'Kings', seventeen were allocated to Old Oak Common (London), ten to Stafford Road (Wolverhampton), with just three remaining at Laira (Plymouth). However, steam-haulage was regarded as a short-term solution only and in September 1959, orders were placed for the 'Western' class diesels. Monday 10 September 1962 was the first day of full diesel working with the 'Westerns', and that same month also saw thirteen 'Kings' withdrawn, including No. 6022 *King Edward III*. The enhanced service continued until March 1967, when the newly electrified line to Euston took over as the main inter-city route, with the Paddington line then being demoted to a semi-fast service operated from Birmingham New Street.

Opposite page: Both photographs show the Railway Enthusiasts Club 'South Midlander' rail tour of 24 April 1955 at Fenny Compton, in the middle of a journey between Banbury and the Stratford-upon-Avon and Midland Junction Railway's station at Stratford. Despite the fact that both the GWR and SMJR stations were adjacent at Fenny Compton, there was no direct connection between the two systems, and they were only joined indirectly by a link through a siding. The tour locomotive was 'Dukedog' 4-4-0 No. 9015, and allocated to Oxford, where the trip began; however, despite much research, your author has not found written proof regarding the use of Northampton-allocated 4F 0-6-0 No. 44186. From looking at the track layout diagram for Fenny Compton, it seems the indirect link between the two systems was not long enough to take a four-coach train plus its locomotive, so presumably No. 44186 was present to help with getting the tour across the link by assisting with splitting and reforming of the train. The first photograph shows No. 9015 in the GWR siding, the link to the SMJR system can be seen on the right with someone in authority standing close by. The second shows the reformed special at Fenny Compton's up SMJR platform (although this is a down train) with a locomotive at either end.

SPECIAL TRIP-3rd
APRIL 24th, 1955
RAILWAY ENTHUSIASTS CLUB
"THE SOUTH MIDLANDER"
Oxford to Kingham, Chipping Norton,
Adderbury, Banbury South, Fenny Compton
(L.M.), Stratford-upon-Avon, Broom Jct.
Evesham, Moreton-in-Marsh, Shipston-on-
Stour, Kingham, Yarnton and Oxford.
(W)
For Conditions see over

23

This is the view looking west about a mile or so to the east of Fenny Compton station, and taken from the A423 road bridge. The two tracks on the right are the GWR main line, while the single track to the left is the SMJR; the Oxford Canal also runs parallel here, but is out of sight. This 9F 2-10-0 is making its way from Stratford to Woodford Halse over the SMJR and, although the locomotive's number is not visible, it is from the early 9200x series. The date is believed to be the spring of 1960, and by this time, the SMJR was freight only, as the passenger service had been withdrawn in 1952 (the GWR station remaining open for passengers until 1964). Fenny Compton saw a significant change to the track layout in 1960, in particular the considerable freight traffic over the GWR route had been creating problems for timetable planners with the fast passenger service. Slow and heavy iron ore trains from Banbury to South Wales were routed over the GWR tracks through here and then onwards, via Hatton Bank, to Stratford. It was decided to divert them over the SMJR from Fenny Compton to Stratford. Among other things, this involved building a new double-track twenty-two-chains-long link at Stratford, a direct connection between the two systems here (visible on page 22), and a new marshalling yard at Honeybourne; this new way of operating was first worked throughout in June 1960. In the middle distance on the GWR lines, a crossing can just be made out between the up and down tracks—this was part of Fenny Compton's new track layout. Despite all the investment, iron ore came to be imported instead and, by the spring of 1965, the SMJR was shut from here to Stratford (apart from the link to the nearby MOD depot that is still in use today).

By April 1960, and after the final 9F 2-10-0s had been built, Banbury shed had an allocation of thirteen of these powerful locomotives. The class regularly worked iron ore services to South Wales and Bilston in the West Midlands. In 1963, Banbury shed was transferred to the London Midland Region and, in 1965, with the closure of the Great Central for through-freight trains, redundant 9Fs arrived from Annesley. It is the summer of 1966 and No. 92030 is passing westbound through Banbury with what appears to be an iron ore working. The locomotive is one of those transferred from Annesley and displays the LMR shed code for Banbury (2D), as well as two service modifications. Firstly, and mainly to those overhauled at Crewe, the original small steps at the front of the smokebox (page 90) were replaced by the continuous wide footstep just visible in the shadow; this was far safer for the crew when dealing with lamps and smokebox door handles. All 9Fs were built with the small steps, but the modification was begun within a few weeks of the last engine being built in 1960. Secondly, the upper lamp bracket, instead of being centrally placed above the number plate and handrail, has been lowered and displaced to the driver's side of the smokebox; also, the central lower bracket was repositioned under the newly-positioned top bracket to maintain the correct configuration. This was done for safety reasons when working on lines with overhead electrification. By the summer of 1966, Banbury's allocation of 9Fs was sixteen, and there were still iron ore workings to both Bilston and Croes Newydd (presumably for Brymbo steelworks), but, between August and the end of steam at Banbury in October 1966, all were transferred away. No. 92030 eventually ended up at Wakefield and from there, it was withdrawn in February 1967.

The end of 1965 effectively signalled the end of steam working over the Western Region of BR, but one through-passenger service a day (except Sundays) from York to Bournemouth and Poole continued with steam over the WR. It arrived diesel-hauled at Banbury, having travelled over the Great Central route, but here changed to steam for the rest of the journey to the South Coast. This involved travelling over WR tracks through Oxford and Reading West before gaining the Southern Region on the line to Basingstoke, the SR continuing with steam until July 1967. By the summer of 1966, the service was largely worked by 'Black 5s', as it is in the first photograph, with No. 45493 ready to depart Banbury (the suffix General was used from 1949–69). This locomotive had been allocated here in the autumn of 1965 and was a popular choice on the service as it was recently ex-works and in good condition; it would arrive back from the coast the following day. Some five miles south of Banbury is Aynho Junction, which is seen in the second photograph dating from Thursday, 1 September 1966; the last steam working on the Bournemouth and Poole service was two days later. No. 44876 (Wolverhampton, Oxley-allocated) is passing under the flyover used by Paddington to Birmingham (via Bicester) services as it heads towards its first stop at Oxford.

By the end of summer 1965, it was becoming increasingly difficult to see GWR 4-6-0s on express passenger workings, the through Poole to York service being an exception. Oxford-allocated No. 6957 *Norcliffe Hall*, in the first photograph, has just arrived at Banbury from the south in typical 1965 condition, missing its nameplates. The GWR 4-6-0s had these removed earlier in the year for safekeeping as there had been cases of theft. A member of the train crew is descending the steps from No. 6957's cab to uncouple the locomotive, which will then retire to Banbury shed, a diesel locomotive taking the train on northwards.

Although by 1966, 'Black 5s' predominated on the Poole to York service as far as Banbury, other locomotives were sometimes seen. The colour view was taken on 21 July 1966 and shows SR-allocated No. 34001 *Exeter* in the bay at the north end of Banbury station; it had worked in from the south earlier that day and was now acting as station pilot. Around this time, *The Railway Observer* reported a number of 'Black 5' failures at the Bournemouth end; this is most likely the reason for the appearance of No. 34001.

The engine shed at Banbury was about twenty chains south of the station and adjacent to the down main line. It had opened in 1908 and was in the Wolverhampton Division, at nationalisation, seventy-nine locomotives were allocated here. This photograph was taken at around 6.15 p.m. on Thursday 29 September 1966, the shed closing over that coming weekend. Latterly, reallocations had reduced the stud to thirteen locomotives (including two stored) to cover the workings: these thirteen were made up of four 'Black 5s', one Ivatt Class 2, and eight 9Fs. On 29 September, there were six locomotives on shed of which three are visible here. On the right is 'Black 5' No. 45437, displaying its 12A shed code, a long way from its home depot of Carlisle Kingmoor. In the middle is 8F No. 48414; one of those built at Swindon works in the Second World War, it has stencilled on both its buffer beam and smoke box door 'COLK'— Colwick, Nottingham. The direct route back to No. 48414's allocated shed had closed earlier that month—the Great Central—and it would be withdrawn in the October. On the left is Ivatt Class 2 2-6-0 No. 46522, a locomotive that spent much of its life in Central Wales and had only been allocated to Banbury two months earlier. Its duties were: the morning freight to Burton Dassett (the MOD depot on the remaining stub of SMJR from Fenny Compton), an afternoon freight to Adderbury, and occasional forays to Bletchington cement works. *The Railway Observer* of June 1965 reported that No. 46522 had been involved in high speed trials on 22 March and reached 82 mph. Other locomotives present on Banbury shed but not visible were Nos 44914, 92213, and 92228; the Banbury station pilot was No. 44944.

This is Banbury's other railway station at Merton Street; it had opened a few months before the nearby GWR station. In 1847, under direction of the London and North Western Railway, two earlier companies (the Oxford and Bletchley Junction and the Buckingham and Brackley Junction) were dissolved and vested in the newly incorporated Buckinghamshire Railway, and the line opened from Bletchley to Banbury Merton Street on 1 May 1850. The Buckinghamshire Act gave the LNWR power to lease the line, and this was done in 1852, then, in 1879, the company was dissolved and vested in the LNWR. It was not a line of importance and could never compete against the GWR for Banbury traffic. From 1901 to 1916, a through carriage to and from London Euston was run, slipped at Bletchley in the down direction, and for a few years after the Grouping a through service was restored. From 1872 until 1953 (1951 for passengers), a connecting line ran to Towcester on the SMJR that diverged off the Buckingham route at Cockley Brake Junction. Passenger services in 1919 were four towards Buckingham (one on Sundays) and two towards Towcester (no Sunday service). While passenger services may have been sparse, the freight traffic was more substantial. In 1938, it was proposed to amalgamate both stations at Banbury, but the Second World War stopped this. The wooden station building was frugally built with an island platform and originally the overall roof had glass panels. In 1956 the station received a facelift, giving an open-plan feel to it prior to the introduction of an experimental diesel railcar service using single units to try and improve the economics of rural branch lines (previously two-car units were the BR-built minimum formation). The photograph plus two half tickets both date from 24 September 1960. The single railcars are coupled together, forming a Buckingham service, and just visible are wooden steps up to the railcar due to the low platform.

Above: The passenger service between Banbury Merton Street and Buckingham may have ceased on and from Monday 2 January 1961, but this was not the case for freight traffic. Looking towards Buckingham in the summer of 1966, this is the LNWR station at Brackley, and freight continued along the branch through here until 2 December 1963, although it lasted at both Merton Street (across the link from the GWR side) and Buckingham (from Verney Junction) until 1966. This station was renamed Brackley Town in 1950 to distinguish it from the Great Central station in Brackley that we will visit later in this book. The change of name does not seem to have been fully implemented: for instance, the summer 1958 LMR timetable still refers to this station as just Brackley. As seen earlier at Merton Street, Brackley had low platforms, and portable wooden steps were on hand for passengers. *The Railway Observer* of April 1966 states that the branch was specially re-opened on 16 February 1966 to enable a privately owned diesel shunter to travel under its own power from Brackley to Buckingham, *en route* to Hams Hall power station. Adjacent to Brackley goods yard were the works of R. Fenwick & Co., who bought, sold, and hired locomotives; the particular locomotive concerned was pre-war ex-LMS 0-6-0 No. 7063. Track lifting was underway along the branch by February 1967, and nothing survives of the station nowadays, as it is lost under modern-day development.

Opposite page: Both photographs date from 24 September 1960 and show firstly the view looking back towards Buckingham from a Banbury-bound service. There used to be double-track over this bridge to Buckingham goods yard, the only double-track on the branch, but it was removed during the First World War. The connecting service on to Bletchley in Buckingham's up platform is in the hands of locally-allocated No. 84002. Both the steam and diesel services had to move to opposite platforms after arrival; the second photograph shows the two single-car DMUs coming in to Buckingham's down platform prior to departure back to Banbury. Before the Banbury to Buckingham service was dieselised experimentally in 1956 and new low-cost halts opened at Radclive and Water Stratford, the steam push-pull workings had been losing £14,000 annually, and receipts were no more than £50 monthly. The railcars boosted income five or six-fold depending on the season, and reduced operating costs by around £300 monthly. Nevertheless, even in the best month of the entire experiment, there was still a deficit, and the annual loss could not be reduced to below £4,700. The Banbury to Buckingham service was due to be withdrawn from 4 January 1960 but survived for another year; following this, these single-car DMUs were used between Buckingham and Bletchley until this also ceased in 1964.

The Buckinghamshire Railway that we followed from Banbury Merton Street also built a line from Verney Junction (although the station of that name did not exist until 1868) towards Oxford, which opened in 1850. These views are at Bicester, the most important intermediate station between Bletchley and Oxford, both are looking towards Bletchley; these pictures are believed to have been taken on Saturday, 30 December 1967, just before closure to passengers. The station opened as Bicester, but changed to Bicester London Road in 1954. Latterly, the station was under WR control, the station seat on the Oxford-bound platform being a WR example. The signal box is Bicester No. 1 and held the hand-wheel that operated the crossing gates. The siding to the left before the gates gave access to a horse dock, the main goods yard being at the other end of the station. The station re-opened to passengers in 1987 as Bicester Town, the terminus of a shuttle from Oxford that continued until closure in 2014. This was to allow for upgrading of the line in connection with the new Chiltern Railways service (October 2015) from Oxford to London Marylebone via the newly-built connection at Bicester, between the GWR and LNWR routes. This station is now called Bicester Village after the nearby shopping outlet.

Launton was the first station east of Bicester and one of the most basic we will visit along this route; it was just short of one mile from the village of Launton. Both views are thought to be taken on the last day this small station remained open for business, Saturday, 30 December 1967 (the date of this ticket). The cream building on the extreme left is the Ladies Waiting Room and toilet, next to it are the signalling instruments seen in close up in the second photograph and at one time enclosed in a small hut. The up (Bletchley-bound) platform edging used some old stone 'sleeper blocks' and the first one to the left of the wooden boarding has two holes just visible on its top, while the down platform was of timber construction. Noticeable on both platforms are the wooden steps needed at Launton due to its low platforms. The station house is deceptive: it might appear to be single-story, but is in fact built up from the ground alongside the embankment, and includes the ticket office abutting onto the platform. The station lamps still burned oil in 1967, heating was by coal, drinking water was delivered from Bicester station in 5-gallon cans, and there was a well in the garden for non-potable water.

Above and opposite: Another two photographs along the line from Bicester to Bletchley, this time at Claydon and again believed taken just before closure on 30 December 1967. The main station buildings were on the up side, where the noticeably narrow platform was constructed of brick and stone, and also another example of a low platform. The down platform can be seen in the Introduction (page 11), this one was wooden with just a single shelter for passengers and of standard height. To the left, the station house adjoined the platform buildings, while to the right, the cottages alongside the goods yard were built by the railway company for its employees. They still remain today. Initially, only the section from Bletchley to Claydon was double-track, this station opening in 1850, with the section on from Claydon towards Oxford being doubled in 1854. As at Launton, an oil lamp is prominent on the up platform. The service along this route between Oxford and Cambridge came under scrutiny in 1959, but local pressure succeeded in winning a reprieve and a DMU service started in the November of that year. Close examination of the timetable for the service at stations between Bicester and Bletchley (both exclusive) reveals it is actually the one in operation until 5 March 1967.

BRITISH RAILWAYS

 TRAIN DEPARTURES *12th JUNE 1966 to 5 MARCH 1967*

from

LAUNTON, MARSH GIBBON & POUNDON, CLAYDON, VERNEY JUNCTION, WINSLOW, SWANBOURNE

WEEKDAYS ONLY

TO BLETCHLEY, BEDFORD ST. JOHNS and CAMBRIDGE

LAUNTON depart	MARSH GIBBON AND POUNDON depart	CLAYDON depart	VERNEY JUNCTION depart	WINSLOW depart	SWANBOURNE depart	
06 50	06 54	07 02	07 06	07 11	07 15	To Bletchley for all stations to Bedford St. Johns
08 21	08 24	08 31	08 36	08 41	08 46	All stations except Bow Brickhill, Aspley Guise and Kempston Hardwick to Cambridge
11 57	12 01	12 08	12 12	12 17	12 21	To Bletchley for all stations to Bedford St. Johns
14 58	15 03	15 09	15 13	15 18	15 23	All stations except Bow Brickhill, Aspley Guise, Stewartby and Kempston Hardwick to Cambridge
17 45	17 49	17 56	18 00	18 05	18 09	To Bletchley for all stations to Bedford St. Johns and for (SO) all stations except Old North Road and Lord's Bridge to Cambridge
19 15	19 19	19 26	19 30	19 35	19 39	To Bletchley, Bedford St. Johns and Cambridge. Change at Bletchley for all stations except Bow Brickhill, Aspley Guise, Stewartby, Kempston Hardwick and Lord's Bridge to Cambridge
23 15sx	...	23 24sx	...	23 31sx	23 36sx	To Bletchley
23 24so	23 28so	23 35so	...	23 42so	23 46so	To Bletchley

TO OXFORD

SWANBOURNE depart	WINSLOW depart	VERNEY JUNCTION depart	CLAYDON depart	MARSH GIBBON AND POUNDON depart	LAUNTON depart	
...	05 45	...	...	...	...	To Bicester London Road, Islip and Oxford
07 48	07 52	07 56	08 00	08 06	08 10	All stations to Oxford
09 35	09 39	09 43	09 47	09 53	09 57	
...	12 04	...	...	...	...	To Bicester London Road and Oxford
14 05	14 09	14 13	14 17	14 23	14 27	
16 03	16 07	16 11	16 15	16 21	16 25	All stations to Oxford
17 16	17 20	17 24	17 27	17 33	17 37	
21 05sx	21 09sx	21 13sx	21 17sx	...	...	To Bicester London Road, Islip and Oxford
21 25so	21 29so	21 33so	21 37so	21 43so	21 47so	All stations to Oxford
22 25	22 29	...	22 35	...	...	To Bicester London Road and Oxford

NOTES

SX—SATURDAYS EXCEPTED   SO—SATURDAYS ONLY   *—SECOND CLASS ONLY

TELEPHONE NUMBERS

LAUNTON — STRATTON AUDLEY 226
MARSH GIBBON and POUNDON — STRATTON AUDLEY 245
CLAYDON — STEEPLE CLAYDON 259

VERNEY JUNCTION — WINSLOW 13
WINSLOW — WINSLOW 21
SWANBOURNE — WINSLOW 31

NO SUNDAY SERVICE

36

Above, below, and opposite: Although the line to Banbury Merton Street branched off the route from Bletchley to Oxford close to the site of where Verney Junction station would eventually be built, no station existed here until 1868. Until then, all changes between the two routes were made at Winslow. It was the opening of the Aylesbury and Buckingham Railway in 1868 from the south that brought about Verney Junction station. The junction became a railway crossroads constructed in the middle of a field with access over a dirt track and little habitation nearby. The Metropolitan Railway bought the ailing Aylesbury & Buckingham in 1891, and in 1910 purchased two Pullman cars that provided a service from here over the 50 miles or so to Baker Street in London. In 1933, the Metropolitan became part of London Transport and it was decided trains north of Aylesbury could not be justified, so they ceased in 1936 (although a limited wartime worker's service was run). All three photographs are thought to be taken on Saturday, 30 December 1967. Firstly, the view towards Oxford with the closed LNWR Verney Junction signal box in the background on the right. By this time, the Buckingham branch had closed completely (1966) and the goods yard here had also been shut (1964), so there was no longer any need for signalling. Verney Junction was the largest station between Oxford and Bletchley and had three platform faces. The Metropolitan trains used the by-now-trackless face of the island platform in the second photograph, which is again looking towards Oxford. Despite no significant settlement nearby, Verney Junction did remain open for passenger traffic until formal closure on and from 1 January 1968. The current plans to re-open the line through here do not include any thoughts about re-opening this station. The ticket is dated 29 October 1959 and is to either Verney Junction or Newport Pagnell.

Two more photographs believed taken on Saturday, 30 December 1967, this time at Winslow looking east with a down Oxford-bound train in the first view. In the early days, Winslow was regarded as one of the more significant stations; the Banbury and Oxford trains were split and reformed here. On the north or up side, the large waiting room with a prominent chimney at its rear is a reminder of the days when Winslow was an important place for changing trains. The main station buildings were of brick and on the south side of the line was the signal box (thirty-four levers). The station lighting was by gas and the town's gas works were close by. Winslow's freight facilities were withdrawn in May 1967, the last passenger trains called at the end of the year, and the signal box closed in early 1968. Christmas shopper specials were run in the mid-1980s, but the route was closed and mothballed in 1993. There are plans to re-open the line with a new station proposed a little to the west of this one, Winslow could have direct services to Oxford, Milton Keynes, Bedford, Aylesbury, and London; eventually, it may be linked to Cambridge, allowing a direct service between the two university cities for the first time in over fifty years.

The final station seen at the end of 1967, looking east along the line from Bicester, is Swanbourne, the last stopping place before Bletchley. The distance from Oxford to Bletchley was over 30 miles and the summit was just to the east of Swanbourne. The main buildings are seen on the down platform; further along, the huts visible are the parcels room, general waiting room, and gentleman's toilet. Also just visible are the wooden steps for the low platform that displays two construction styles. The door in the main building was permanently secured shut by screws and iron bars following an accident in 1902, when a member of the public walked out in front of a moving train. A timber shelter was the only structure on the up side and where the oil lighting can be seen. The station house, which still stands today, is distinctive and includes conflicting gables with dormer windows. Adjacent to the bicycle and entrance to the booking office is a large sign regarding closure of the route on and from 1 January 1968 (page 63). Between here and Bletchley were the Second World War-built Swanbourne Sidings: following the 1955 Modernisation Plan, it was proposed to expand these into a large marshalling yard, but the idea was later dropped.

We visited Nuneaton on 1 August 1963 and spent the afternoon at the old LNWR station; this had the suffix 'Trent Valley' added from 1924 until after Nuneaton's other station (Abbey Street) closed in 1968. At this time, Nuneaton was in the thick of the West Coast Main Line's 25kV AC overhead electrification work (page 15). From January 1963, electric traction had been inaugurated on some public services between Crewe and Stafford, but it was to be 2 March 1964 before electric working started between Stafford and Nuneaton. The first photograph shows 'Jubilee' No. 45624 *St Helena* shunting in sidings on the east side of the station. By the early 1960s, there was little express work left for the 'Jubilees' and many had been transferred away to see out their time at secondary-type depots such as Nuneaton: five of the class were allocated here in the summer of 1962, yet none at all in January 1959. *St Helena* will be withdrawn from Nuneaton shed in about three months' time. 'Black 5' No. 45186 of Saltley, Birmingham shed (21A) has arrived from the south and looks to have stopped at the station for a crew change. The lamp code on the front indicates an express freight pipe-fitted throughout, with the automatic brake operative on not less than 90 per cent of the vehicles.

To reach Nuneaton on 1 August 1963, we travelled by train from Leamington Spa Avenue; my father's ticket is included. The highlight for your author as a young trainspotter was the appearance of 'Rebuilt Patriot' No. 45529 *Stephenson* hauling another express freight from the south, although, unlike No. 45186 on the previous page, no crew change took place during its stop here. In 1944, the LMS decided that they needed ninety-one locomotives in their 'Class 6' category and this was achieved by continuing the rebuilding of all seventy-one 'Royal Scots' (including No. 46170) plus the two 'Jubilees' rebuilt in 1942. This left a balance of eighteen, which is why only that number of the fifty-two 'Patriots' constructed were rebuilt. No. 45529 was rebuilt in 1947 but not named *Stephenson* until August 1948 at Chesterfield; this was because it was in memory of George Stephenson (of *Rocket* fame), who had died and been buried at Chesterfield 100 years earlier. Ahead of No. 45529 and to the right in the distance is one of the electrification works trains. The signalling was also attended to at the same time as the electrification and a power signal box was built here at the other end of the station. It controlled 17.75 route miles and 62 track miles, including parts of the Ashby, Leicester, and Coventry branches; the box remained in use until 2008. The white diamonds on the signal posts indicate the line is track-circuited, and although No. 45529 is held at the signals, there is no need to contact the signal box and protect the train (Rule 55) as the signalman will already be aware. As for the 'Rebuilt Patriots'—the first withdrawal was in 1961, No. 45529 met its end in 1964, and the final class withdrawal was in 1965.

The LNWR branch from Weedon to Leamington Spa was constructed in two parts. The first section from Weedon to here at Daventry opened in 1888, the second from Daventry onwards to Marton Junction in 1895, where it joined the existing line from Rugby to Leamington Spa. This view is looking towards Leamington and dates from 10 June 1961. The line from Weedon to Marton Junction was single throughout, but the bridges, cuttings, and embankments were built for double-track. Daventry station was mainly constructed of wood and gas-lit, although after the Second World War the station buildings and canopy on the up platform were largely removed. On opening in 1888, the service was six passenger trains each way, but by 1919, five worked to Daventry with three running through to Leamington Spa, and no Sunday service. *The Railway Magazine* of June 1957 commented how poorly patronised the passenger services were, and in the summer of 1958, these comprised just two workings each way through Daventry, with a third on Saturdays, but none on Sundays. One train each way over the branch worked to and from Northampton, involving reversal at Blisworth, but the entire passenger service was withdrawn from 15 September 1958. Goods traffic in 1957 comprised daily pick-up freights in both directions over the branch and workings to Southam cement works, plus there were occasional freight diversions off the West Coast Main Line; total closure at Daventry came about in December 1963.

Enthusiasts are wandering over the West Coast Main Line at Blisworth during the Stephenson Locomotive Society's (SLS) 'SMJR and District' rail tour visit on Saturday, 14 May 1960. The main line here was opened by the London and Birmingham Railway in 1838, but this Blisworth station did not open until 1845, replacing the original station on the Northampton Road. This later station was further to the west and about a mile or so from the village of Blisworth, it was at the junction of the 1845-opened line to Northampton and Peterborough that can be seen branching off to the right. The final railway to arrive here was the precursor of the SMJR in 1866 and this turned off to the left, but is not visible in the photograph. All this made the small station of Blisworth a bustling junction in the early twentieth century. In 1910, it was served by sixty-eight trains daily: sixteen each way to Northampton, ten each way on the main London to Rugby line, four each way on the SMJR to Banbury Merton Street, and four each way on the SMJR to Stratford-upon-Avon. Passenger volume was such that the station bookstall employed several boys to carry trays of chocolates, cigarettes, and newspapers for sale to passengers at their carriage windows. Opposite the station was the Blisworth Station Hotel, doing a good trade with passengers awaiting connections. However, the world was a different place by the date of this photograph and Blisworth station had closed to passengers four months earlier from 4 January; the Station Hotel still exists, but is now the Walnut Tree Inn.

The Gloucestershire Railway Society's 'SMJR, Wolverton & Oxford Road Jct' trip of 11 May 1957 is seen at Towcester, both photographs being taken from the station's footbridge (the only one on the SMJR). The tall signal box in the first view dated from 1910 and used to be directly connected to the footbridge; previously there were two boxes at Towcester (East and West). In the distance, the line splits—Blisworth to the left and Ravenstone Wood Junction, Olney, to the right. The locomotive is Gloucester-allocated LMS 2P 4-4-0 No. 40540. Some of the remaining station buildings as well as the water tower can be seen in the second view looking to the south-west; in this direction, there used to be (from 1910) two parallel single lines to Banbury and Stratford that went their different ways at the site of Green's Norton Junction. The various passenger services ceased as follows: Olney as early as 1893, Banbury Merton Street in 1951, and Blisworth to Stratford in 1952. The missing track adjacent to the rail tour had recently been removed and a goods service carried on through Towcester (Blisworth to Woodford Halse) until the beginning of February 1964.

The SMJR was formed through the coming together of four railway companies: the East and West Junction Railway; the Evesham, Redditch and Stratford-upon-Avon Railway; the Stratford-upon-Avon, Towcester and Midland Junction Railway (all 1 January 1909); and the Northampton and Banbury Junction Railway (1 July 1910). At its furthest west, the SMJR connected with the Midland Railway at Broom Junction and it also connected with the MR at its furthest east, Ravenstone Wood Junction, Olney. The SMJR thus provided a link between the MR main line from St Pancras, London and their line to Bristol in the west, avoiding the long deviation north of Birmingham. The final part of this link was that from Towcester to Ravenstone Wood Junction (three miles or so to the west of Olney) on the MR line from Northampton to Bedford, and it opened in 1891.

All three photographs were taken in October 1959 at Roade: here, the line from Towcester to Ravenstone Wood crossed over the LNWR main line from London Euston. First is the view along the LNWR main line towards London, taken from the footbridge seen in the final photograph. The lattice-girder bridge crossing the main line carries the railway from Towcester to Ravenstone Wood; between the bridge and the large water tower (that still stands today) are a line of wagons. The signal box is Roade Junction. A link between the two systems ran through the arch at the right of the footbridge in the final photograph and then to the right of the signal box. The second photograph in the opposite direction from the same footbridge shows Roade station, the bay on the left for the connecting spur having been filled in. No passenger services used the spur, its function being solely the transfer of goods traffic; it closed in 1917.

Another special we travelled on was the SLS 'Tour of Seven Branch Lines' on 14 April 1962. The tour locomotive from Birmingham New Street was LMS 2P 4-4-0 No. 40646 of Bescot shed (21B) that was withdrawn the following month. This was the last year for the class; in fact, by the end of 1962, the entire stock of 4-4-0s on BR had been withdrawn—on 31 December 1949, there had been 1,354 in service. Both photographs are taken at Northampton Castle station, where an assistant locomotive was coupled behind the 2P in the form of Bedford-allocated Fowler Class 3 2-6-2 tank No. 40026. The pair will then traverse the Northampton to Bedford line that had closed to passengers the month previously. Seventy Fowler Class 3 2-6-2Ts had been constructed during 1930–32, but by the beginning of 1962, the class was down to single figures. They were described by locomotive designer E. S. Cox as 'one of the feeblest of modern times'. An attempt had been made to improve their steaming; these large outside steam pipes were fitted plus the chimney was moved forward. Most noticeably different were the twenty so-called 'Condensers'; these were fitted with exhaust pipes conveying steam back to the water tanks, including No. 40026, and they worked to Moorgate, London via the 'widened lines'.

The first station to open in Northampton was Bridge Street in 1845 on the L&BR cross-country line from Blisworth to Peterborough. In the early 1840s, the direct Great Northern line from Peterborough to London that is nowadays part of the East Coast Main Line did not exist. So, although in our eyes it may seem a curious routing from Peterborough via Northampton, and Wolverton to London, at the time, it was promoted quite heavily. The 47 miles from Blisworth to Peterborough only took one year to build, and by March 1846, the L&BR was advertising through merchandise trains from Peterborough to the capital. These two views at Northampton Bridge Street both date from Thursday, 1 March 1962: in the first, B1 No. 61223 of Lincoln shed (40A) is hauling the 12.40 p.m. from Peterborough East to Northampton Castle, this route's passenger service surviving until May 1964. The second photograph shows the 1.35 p.m. push-pull train from Bedford Midland Road enshrouded in steam and ready to leave for Northampton Castle; this line losing its passenger service over that coming weekend. The locomotive is BR Standard Class 2 2-6-2T No. 84006 and allocated to Bedford at this time. The date of the ticket is 21 February 1961.

The Act for the Bedford and Northampton Railway was passed on 5 July 1865, but further Acts were required to extend the time needed for completion. The line had its own terminus at Northampton St John's Street, but at the Bedford end, it ran to the MR station; it opened throughout in June 1872. Under the terms of the Act, the MR worked the line initially for a proportion of the receipts and in 1885, it came under MR control. The first intermediate station after departing Northampton was Piddington, where this view looking to the north-west dates from 1 March 1962. The initial service was five trains daily each way by 1919: this was six to Northampton and five back to Bedford; there was no Sunday service. In 1939, St John's Street closed and the service was diverted through Bridge Street to Northampton Castle. The summer 1958 timetable shows five services each way from Monday to Friday that increased to seven on Saturdays, but again nothing on Sundays. The February 1959 issue of *Trains Illustrated* reported that DMUs introduced the previous summer had attracted more than double the number of passengers compared to the previous steam-worked service. However, at the end of May 1961, notice was given of the intention to withdraw the passenger service, and this duly came to pass on and from Monday, 5 March 1962. One big change in those last months of the passenger service was that Bedford's two-car DMU sets were taken out of service in December 1961 due to fatigue on the axle wheel seats, and steam was brought back to fill the breach. Freight carried on over the full length of the branch until 1964, after which it served just the MOD depot near Piddington from the Northampton end. The ticket is dated 26 October 1961.

The next station towards Bedford was Olney and again both photographs (and this ticket) date from 1 March 1962. The first is looking east, with the goods yard on the right and signal box in the centre: there were once exchange sidings at Olney to handle SMJR traffic on their line from Towcester to Ravenstone Wood Junction. On the extreme left is Olney's 50-foot diameter turntable and further to the left, out of sight, is a small engine shed; these were used by engines off the SMJR, but saw little use after closure of this route in the 1950s. In addition to the normal freight service, there were 'Banana Specials' run through Olney from Avonmouth Docks, Bristol to the Fyffes' depot at Somers Town, London. These were worked by the SMJR and MR (and later the LMS), and they ran in competition with the much shorter GWR route. There were paths in the Working Timetable departing Avonmouth at 12.30 p.m., 1.55 p.m., and 4.15 p.m. The second photograph shows No. 84006 propelling its train towards Northampton. In 1865, powers were obtained for a line from Newport Pagnell to Olney but, although construction began, it was never completed; some of the earthworks still exist today.

Another branch visited just before closure was that from Wolverton to Newport Pagnell. Newport Pagnell had been reached in 1817 by a branch from the Grand Junction Canal at Great Linford; it was 1.25 miles long with seven locks. The Newport Pagnell Railway obtained their Act in 1863 and purchased this short canal for £9,000, although the railway as built did not directly follow the line of the canal. At Newport Pagnell, the railway reused several canal warehouses plus the Shipley Wharf. The first locomotive traversed the line in 1865, freight traffic began in 1866, and it opened from Wolverton for passengers in September 1867. This photograph was taken on 20 August 1964 (also the date of the tickets) and shows No. 41222 about to propel its two coaches back to Wolverton. No. 41222 had arrived with four coaches on a late afternoon service packed mostly with employees from the railway works at Wolverton; two of these coaches were then shunted into the goods yard beyond the station (the old Shipley Wharf) for use the following morning. The station consisted of a single platform with canopy; just visible at this end, by the signal, is an open ground frame on a raised plinth that controlled access to the sidings. Behind the photographer used to be an engine shed, which had closed in 1955.

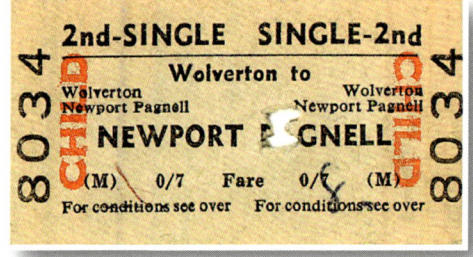 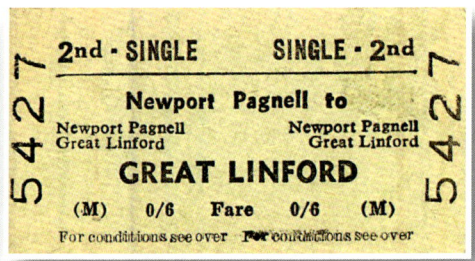

Two more photographs along the branch from Newport Pagnell to Wolverton, but this time taken on 1 March 1962 (the ticket is dated 20 August 1964). It is just after 4 p.m. and the first shows a push-pull service being propelled to Wolverton crossing the Grand Union Canal (previously the Grand Junction Canal). There were two intermediate stations along the branch—one at Great Linford, and one here at Bradwell, where the view is looking towards Newport Pagnell. In the early days, there had been proposals to extend the line beyond Newport Pagnell to join the Northampton to Bedford route at Olney, and even beyond, to a junction with the line from Northampton to Wellingborough, but these were never completed. In 1875, it became part of the LNWR. The branch may have had a very different history had a proposal mentioned in the 13 May 1904 issue of *Engineering* come about; this was to electrify the line with a similar system to that used by the Lancashire and Yorkshire Railway between Liverpool and Southport. In 1919, there were nine down and ten up passenger services, by the summer of 1958, this had become six down (eight on Saturdays) and seven up (nine on Saturdays), but no Sunday service. The last passenger trains ran on Saturday, 5 September 1964, with freight continuing until May 1967.

52

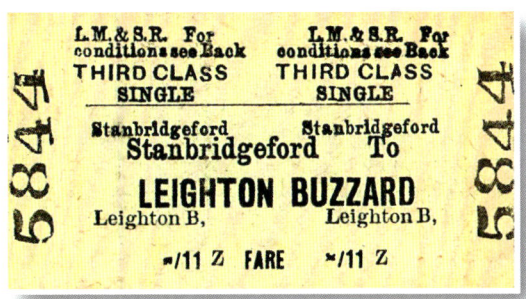

Above and opposite page: Another much earlier connection to the West Coast Main Line was that from Leighton Buzzard to Dunstable; this had been authorised under the Dunstable, London and Birmingham Railway Act of 1845, and the double-track branch opened in June 1848. Both views are at Leighton Buzzard, and the first shows the railway infrastructure to the south of the station on Sunday, 8 October 1961. On the far left is an old LNWR London inner-suburban Oerlikon electric unit, now used as a mess coach. Inside the shed, one of the branch's 2-6-2Ts is barely visible, while the Dunstable branch can be seen curving behind to the east. The long line of loaded chalk wagons in the middle of the photograph will have come from Totternhoe Quarry on the Dunstable branch, many of these went north to Southam Cement Works. On the far right, the two-coach push-pull set for the branch was stabled in a short siding in the middle of the four WCML tracks. In the late 1950s, there had been rebuilding at Leighton Buzzard station, which can be seen in the colour photograph taken on Saturday, 30 June 1962 (also the date of the LMS ticket); this was the last day of the branch passenger service and shows No. 41222 preparing for the very final departure to Dunstable at 5.38 p.m. (see also page 13).

Above and opposite: Both photographs date from the last day of passenger services between Leighton Buzzard and Dunstable—30 June 1962. No. 41222 is standing in the loco siding on the exit from Leighton Buzzard engine shed seen previously, but this locomotive had a tragic side to its history that was reported in *The Railway Magazine* of February 1956. At about 8.40 a.m. on 20 April 1955, while working the morning service from Luton Bute Street to Leighton Buzzard, a fierce blowback occurred. Normally, air is drawn in from the locomotive cab through the firebox door, but a blowback occurs when the flow of air is reversed and instead flames come out of the firebox and envelope the locomotive cab. This forced the enginemen off the footplate—the driver suffered shock and burns, but the fireman was fatally injured. With nobody now in charge of No. 41222, speed increased and it ran non-stop through both Dunstable Town and North stations, the porter-guard travelling in the rear compartment of the push-pull set eventually making a full brake application. Tunnels can be one of the causes of blowbacks by restricting the flow of gases out of the chimney, but there were none locally. Drivers and firemen were taught how to try and stop blowbacks occurring; nevertheless, they did happen occasionally and there were twenty-three nationally during 1955, but this one was exceptionally violent. (*Paul Cowley*)

There was just the single station between Leighton Buzzard and Dunstable North, here at Stanbridgeford. The monochrome photograph was taken on Sunday, 8 October 1961 looking eastwards, while the colour view is another dating from the last day of the branch passenger service—30 June 1962—and is of the very final arrival from Leighton Buzzard pulling in to the station. Although only ten years of age at the time, my father dropped me off at Stanbridgeford and then drove to Dunstable North to film proceedings there, each of us using both still and cine cameras. After a wait of about thirty minutes, I then caught the final working back to Leighton Buzzard using this child's ticket, where we met up again; I am sure in today's world, this sort of parental behaviour would be much frowned upon. A lasting impression of Stanbridgeford station was just how strangely decrepit it looked, and it appears I was not the only person who thought this way. Part of an episode of that 1960s TV classic *The Avengers* was filmed here (Producer Brian Clemens lived in the area). I am not aware of a family connection between us, although Brian Clemens claimed relationship to author Mark Twain (Samuel Longhorn Clemens) as did my grandfather; certainly, my great-grandfather was near-identical in looks to Mark Twain.

When the line from Leighton Buzzard opened in 1848, it was to a different Dunstable station, replaced by the one visible here in 1866, allowing onward connection to Luton, the original station then becoming a goods depot. This replacement station was called Dunstable, changing to Dunstable North in 1950, and is another seen on 30 June 1962 (also the date of the ticket). No. 41222 is propelling the 5.38 p.m. final working from Leighton Buzzard into Dunstable North's bay platform with some 270 passengers crammed in. It had acquired a wreath from the South Bedfordshire Locomotive Club, a 'Final Dasher' headboard, plus also various banners and slogans including 'The Dashers Last Run—All Because Of Beeching'. The tracks on the right are those that carried on to Luton and Hatfield; passenger services continued from this direction to Dunstable until 1965. On the left is the town's gas works, in front of this, on the platform, a gas lamp can be seen, while to the right the new 1958-built signal box is visible (built because of subsidence affecting the old LNWR box). A 1951 article in *Trains Illustrated* was incredulous that Dunstable, with a population of just over 17,000, had no direct rail service to London. The distance to the capital by rail was some 38 miles, yet the time taken to get there (including change of train *en route*) was never less than ninety minutes. Today, things are far worse as there is no railway, yet Dunstable's population has doubled—surely a prime candidate for reinstatement of the railway. Your author can envisage an interval Thameslink-style service from Brighton, Gatwick Airport, under London to Luton, Dunstable, Leighton Buzzard, and Milton Keynes—perhaps even onwards to Newport Pagnell, with that branch also reinstated. A fantasy world, probably, but you never know.

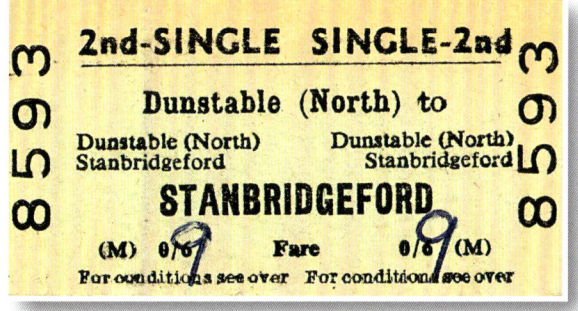

Above and opposite page: Both photographs were taken on 30 June 1962 at Luton Bute Street station, the first to open in the town (1858) and some ten years before the Midland Railway built its station here on the line from London St Pancras; the two were adjacent on opposite sides of Station Road. By 1962, there were only three passenger services each way (none on Sundays) between Leighton Buzzard and Dunstable North, and the first of these ran through to Luton Bute Street. Paul Cowley travelled on this train from Leighton Buzzard behind No. 84002 departing at 7.28 a.m., and the first photograph shows it after arrival at Luton Bute Street. The lattice footbridge behind ran from Midland Road to Bute Street, spanning the two stations and giving access to both. Behind the footbridge is the huge three-story bonded

warehouse inside which ran one of the station's west end sidings; this has now demolished and replaced by student accommodation. The second photograph shows the return working of No. 84002 backing into the station before departure. In the foreground is the shadow of the footbridge, while in the distance can just be seen a gasometer associated with Luton Gas Works. Part of the trackbed of the railway from Luton to Dunstable has been used in the creation of a guided busway that opened in 2013. (*Paul Cowley*)

Above, below, and opposite page: On 26 October 1961, we travelled from Northampton Castle to Hitchin, changing trains at Bedford (Midland Road) where both photographs were taken (and also the date of all three tickets). To your author as a young lad, this station seemed a bit odd, as express services from London St Pancras to Leicester and the north bypassed it a little to the west. This was because the station was built on the original Midland Railway alignment from Leicester through Bedford to Hitchin (opened throughout in 1857), and from there to London King's Cross over Great Northern metals. The entirely MR-owned route from London St Pancras to Bedford did not open until some ten years later and had a curved slow approach to Bedford, hence the route bypassing the station for non-stopping trains. The first photograph is taken under the road bridge at the south end of the station, where the MR 3F is No. 43449, this was Bedford-allocated from December 1959 until withdrawn in September 1962. Note the white background behind the signal on the footbridge to make it visibly stand out. The Hitchin service in the second photograph departed from a bay with a low platform, the gap to the footsteps on the DMU being very noticeable, and a portable set of wooden steps were available on request.

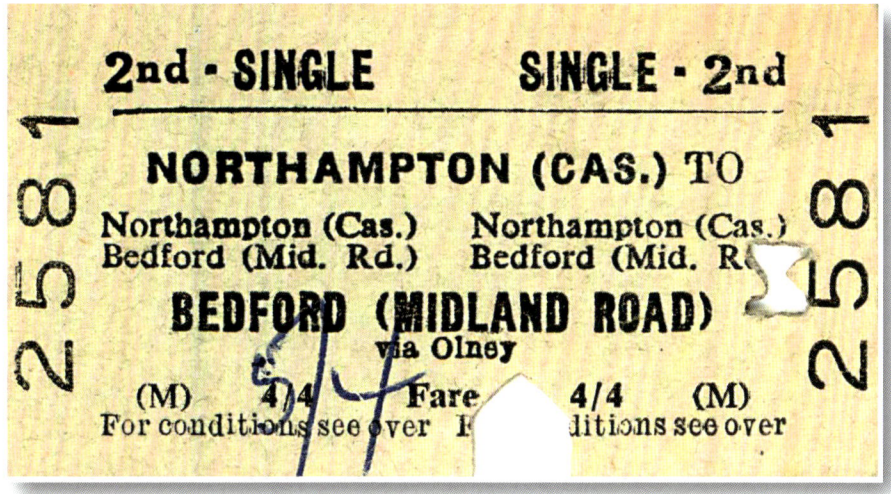

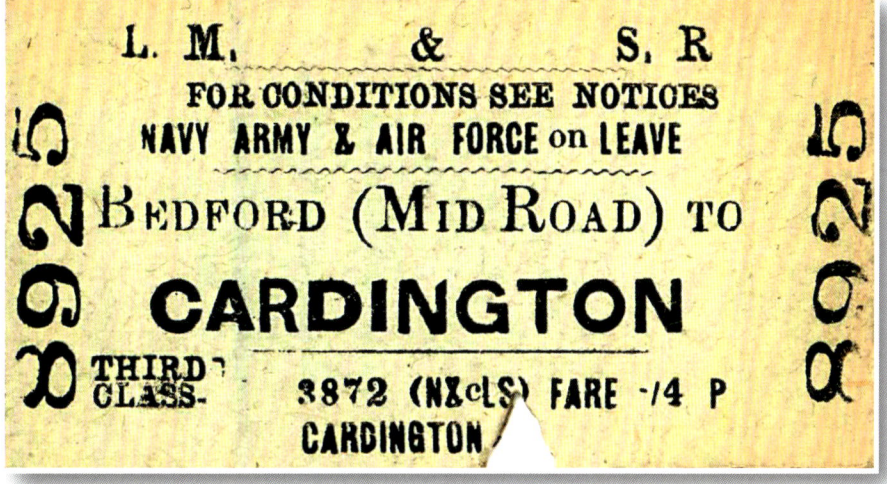

B11

2nd - SPECIAL
CHEAP DAY
SPECIAL - 2nd
CHEAP DAY
7961
Cambridge to
OXFORD
via Bletchley
(W)
Oxford to
CAMBRIDGE
via Bletchley
(W)
7961
For conditions see over

2nd-SINGLE
SINGLE-2nd
2550
CHILD
Bedford (St. Johns) to
Bedford (St. Johns)
Bletchley
Bedford (St. Johns)
Bletchley
BLETCHLEY
CHILD
2550
(M) 1/5 FARE 1/5 (M)
For conditions see over

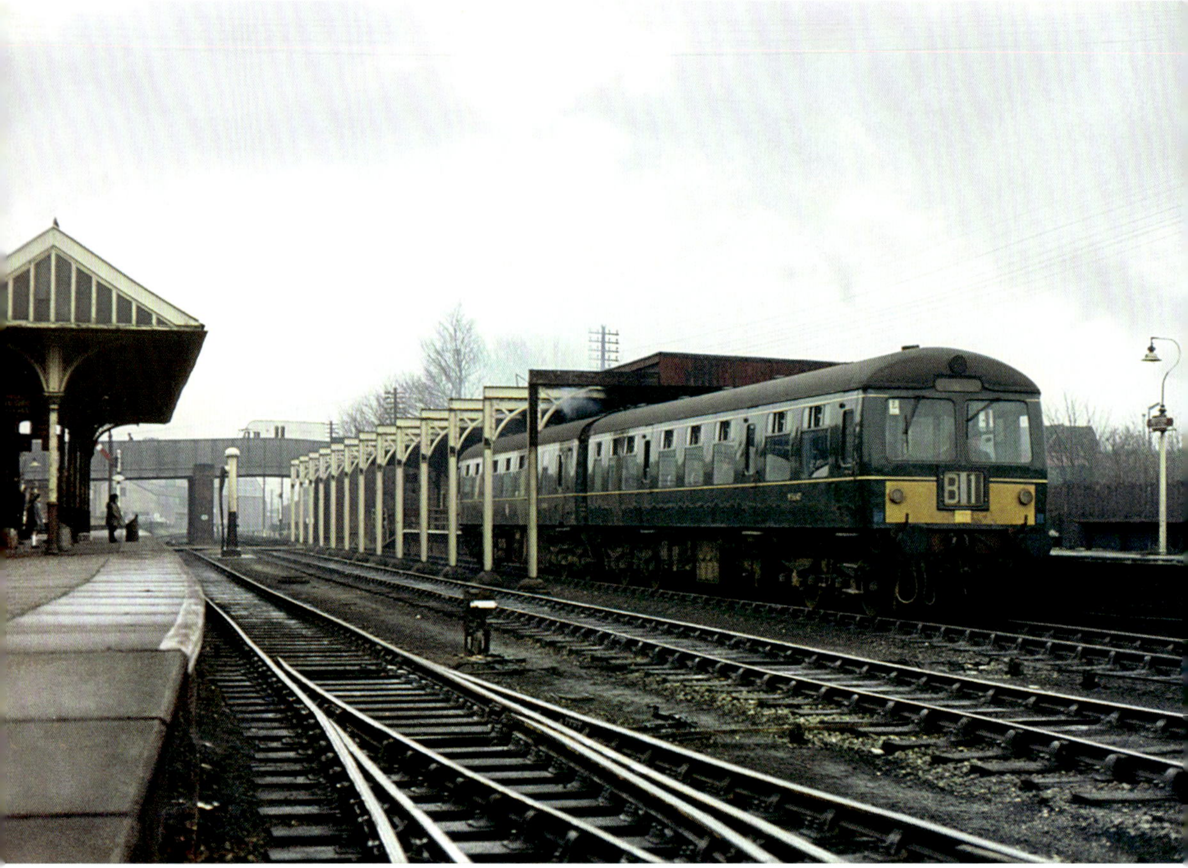

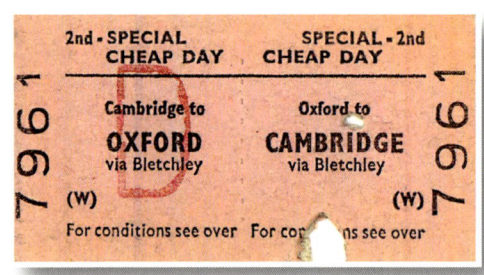

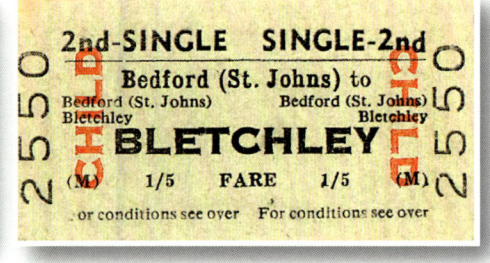

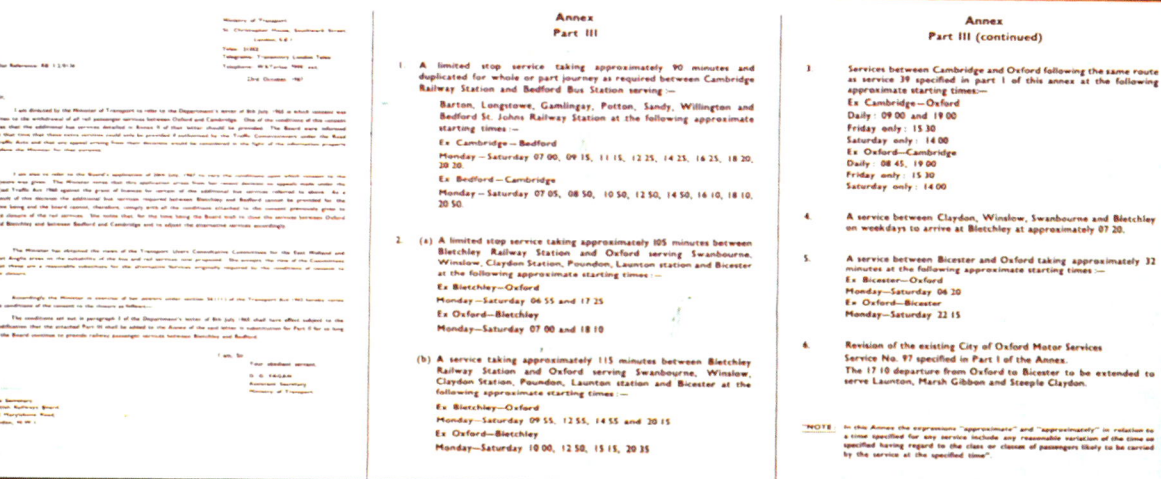

Above and opposite page: Bedford's first station opened in 1846, the eastern terminus of a line from Bletchley that was extended in 1862 by the LNWR to Cambridge; it became Bedford St Johns in 1924. On 27 November 1967, my father and Eric Parker made a return journey from Oxford to Cambridge, the cost of this cheap day return ticket being £1 2s 0d according to Parker's diaries. They stopped off at St Johns, and this view is looking in the Cambridge direction with a Cravens Class 105 DMU bound for Bletchley. This platform is the original and was once covered by a train shed that is now removed, leaving the supporting girders and new flat canopy. The platform on the left opened with the Cambridge extension and has a disused water column opposite its far end. By this time, the closure notices that came in to effect from 1 January 1968 were on display, although the service from Bedford to Bletchley survived as it still does today. This remaining service terminated at Bedford St Johns (unstaffed from July 1968) until May 1984, when a new St Johns station was opened at the north end of a triangle in the goods yard, giving direct access to the main station at Bedford. My child's ticket is dated 29 October 1959.

It is not known exactly when the extraction of iron from its ores was first carried out in the East Midlands, but it was certainly happening well before the Roman invasion. The Roman occupation saw a considerable expansion in production; ironworks are mentioned in the Doomsday Book, and this continued in medieval times. These ores were smelted with charcoal from local forests, but the destruction of woodlands was so vast that it endangered the supply of timber for the navy's ships and laws were passed in certain areas forbidding the making of charcoal. The effect was that the ironmasters moved to areas where the ore was associated with coal deposits, such as South Wales, and ironstone working locally was abandoned for three centuries. Its existence in the East Midlands appears to have been largely forgotten: a book was even published in 1702 denying its presence in Northamptonshire. The rediscovery seems to have been about 1815, but the first real impetus came with the Great Exhibition of 1851, where local samples were shown. Events then followed rapidly and, after discovery of a rich ore bed at Higham Ferrers, the construction of an ironworks at Wellingborough was started in 1852. This photograph dates from 13 July 1967, when my father and friends visited a number of ironstone quarries in the area. Their trip was specifically made to see this particular locomotive working at the Irchester Quarry system near Wellingborough, and where production had started in the 1863. It is 0-4-0 No. 14 and had been built by Manning Wardle in 1912 (W/N 1795), it is seen exiting what is believed to be Lodge Pit. Eric Parker's diaries refer to 'the craziest track imaginable laid on a narrow shelf with a drop into a water filled worked out quarry'. This system closed in 1969, but No. 14 survived to be preserved and is undergoing restoration as this book is being written.

Another ironstone system near Wellingborough was at Finedon; this was originally a horse-worked tramway beginning in 1874, which ran to the Midland Railway. Following the Great Depression, the Wellingborough Ironworks were rebuilt on modern lines as was its transport system; it represented the last sustained attempt nationally to modernise a narrow-gauge ironstone system. Latterly, it was run by Stewart & Lloyds Minerals Ltd, who had taken over from the Stanton Ironworks Co. Ltd in 1950. These photographs were taken on Thursday, 29 September 1966, just a couple of weeks or so before the system shut down. Only one locomotive was in steam this day: 0-6-0 No. 87 built by Peckett's of Bristol in 1942 (W/N 2029); the other two were being prepared for a visit on the Saturday by the Industrial Railway Society. The system was metre-gauge and No. 87 can first be seen with ore being loaded at the quarry. The wagons carried pairs of skips on steel underframes and were taken eight at a time for their contents to be emptied into standard-gauge wagons on an adjacent track in the second photograph. This was done by a crane with lifting chains wrapped around trunnions on the skips, which were then carried across and emptied; the cine film taken on the day shows it to be a quite scary procedure.

This undated view is of Rushden station on the Wellingborough to Higham Ferrers branch, it is taken from the footbridge at the east end of the station looking towards Wellingborough. Trade, especially the boot and shoe business, was expanding in the town, and businessmen were unhappy they had no direct rail link. The Midland Railway obtained an Act in July 1890 and the first passenger service ran from Wellingborough through Rushden to terminate at Higham Ferrers on 1 May 1894, although freight had started the previous September. The branch connected to the main line at Irchester Junction and the distance to Higham Ferrers was 3.5 miles. An electric tram service was also proposed but came to nothing, as were thoughts of extending the railway onwards to Raunds on the MR-owned Kettering to Huntingdon line. The timetable for February 1919 shows ten passenger trains in each direction, but none on Sundays. The freight timetable, operative from 7 May 1945, shows four workings each way plus an extra light engine working from Higham Ferrers to Rushden in the morning, but again, nothing on Sundays. By the summer of 1958, it was still a weekday-only service but now with twelve passenger trains each way, rising to fifteen on Saturdays. The end for the passenger service at Rushden came on and from 15 June 1959, although freight continued until 1969. A notable source of freight traffic well into the 1960s was fruit and sugar for Whitworth Bros. Today, Rushden station has been preserved by the Rushden Historical Transport Society and they operate a heritage railway here—the Rushden, Higham & Wellingborough Railway.

Another undated photograph, possibly taken on the same day as that at Rushden (previous photograph) in the same snowy conditions. This is Irthlingborough looking east from the A6 road bridge. The two stations were relatively close by and before Rushden opened, Irthlingborough was one of its nearest railheads. The railway here is one we have seen before; it was 47 miles long and ran from Blisworth on the London and Birmingham Railway and through Northampton Bridge Street, all the way to Peterborough. This line dated from 1845 and some years before the direct Great Northern route from Peterborough to London opened, thus attracting custom despite its rather indirect link to the capital. To the south-west of the station, a branch was built in 1890 that served a brickworks and tannery, and from 1915 the Ebbw Vale Steel, Iron & Coal Co. Ltd. In the summer of 1918, Ebbw Vale started preparations for iron ore mining on a scale unknown in the Midlands. The ore beds were reached by an adit (tunnel) running north-west; at the Irthlingborough end, they built a large ore-calcining and processing plant (raw ore burnt with coal to raise its ore content). The tunnel eventually emerged by Finedon village, and there were branch lines off the main tunnel to serve the workings. Electric locomotives were used in the 3-foot gauge tunnel system—battery powered at the working galleries and 250V overhead wire elsewhere. To control traffic, a system of signalling by lights was used, and at the tunnel mouth the two outside tracks converged. Latterly, the overhead wire electric locomotives were rebuilt to battery-electric, with most of the batteries carried on separate bogie 'tenders'. Irthlingborough station closed to passengers in May 1964, the mine shut in September 1965, and goods traffic ceased in June 1966.

Above and opposite page: After visiting Irchester (page 64) on 13 July 1967, my father's party moved on to the Kettering area to visit both the Storefield Ironstone system and Cohen's scrapyard. The workings at Storefield had opened in 1898 and its railway system was built to a 2-foot 6-inch gauge that lay to the west of the old A43 (nowadays the A4300) and both north and south of the River Ise. The output went entirely to the Bennerley Furnaces near Ilkeston, Derbyshire, and when these shut down in 1929 the Storefield quarries were closed. The by-no-means exhausted quarries were acquired by the South Durham Steel & Iron Co. Ltd, but lay dormant for about ten years. Shortly after the outbreak of the Second World War, the railway system was rebuilt to standard-gauge and in general followed the course of the earlier narrow-gauge tracks. The route was quite picturesque and Eric Parker's diary talks about 'charming wooden country'.

The rebuilt system opened in May 1940 and all locomotives, with one exception, were second-hand. This exception is the locomotive featuring in both photographs at Storefield—No. 19—built by Andrew Barclay of Kilmarnock in 1940 (W/N 2101). The livery was plain mid-green plus red side-rods, buffer beam, etc., with the locomotive kept in a tidy condition. There were three other locomotives at Storefield on this day: *Enterprise* and No. 20 were both in the shed, while No. 11 was in use bringing empty wagons and taking loaded ones away, complete with an 'L-plate' on its chimney. The last place visited on 13 July 1967 was Cohen's scrapyard near Cransley on the Loddington branch, to the west of Kettering. Numerous steam locomotives met their demise here, even diesel and electric examples. Nearest to the camera is No. 48270, while behind are Nos 76036, 45276, 45240, and 48739.

The largest of all the ironstone railways in the East Midlands (and the whole UK) was at Corby. A thick bed of ore had been discovered while building Corby Tunnel on the Midland Railway line from Kettering to Manton (opened 1879). By the 1960s, the prime function of the Corby system was to supply ore to the local works, although some did go elsewhere. Traffic was heavy, there were sections of double-track, colour light signalling had been introduced where necessary, and there was even a road crossing protected by an automatic warning system. The first photograph is believed to date from 22 May 1965 and shows No. 35 inside Pen Green engine shed, this locomotive had been built by Manning Wardle & Co. Ltd in 1895 (W/N 1317), (see also page 12). The massive depot had been brought into use during August 1954 and had eight parallel roads capable of holding forty locomotives; it was almost directly above Corby Tunnel. The second photograph dates from the Industrial Railway Society 'Farewell to Steam' trip on 23 June 1973, and shows a diesel replacement. Twenty-three ex-BR Class 14 diesels had been purchased by Stewart & Lloyds at the end of 1968 for use around the East Midlands; No. 28 (ex-D9547) had been built at Swindon in July 1965 and was scrapped at Corby in the summer of 1982.

An LNWR branch opened in 1894 connecting Seaton, on the Rugby to Luffenham line, to Uppingham, and this black and white view is looking east from Uppingham towards Seaton in August 1954. On weekdays in February 1919, there were four or five trains each way, and by summer 1958, this had become nine. However, *The Railway Observer* of May 1960 reported traffic that Easter was particularly light, the correspondent being the only passenger; closure to passenger services took place in June 1960, although occasional specials ran in connection with Uppingham public school. The headmaster referred to the withdrawal of passenger services during Speech Day in 1960, although it appears he was more concerned about Boundary Commission proposals that Rutland should lose its identity. Thus, when the RCTS 'Join Lines' tour visited on 18 May 1963, the branch was effectively freight-only. The tour was 'top and tailed' from Seaton, and out of sight at the station was No. 42089, while here by the goods yard was No. 44414. Arrival at Uppingham was dead on time at 5.27 p.m. and departure would have been likewise. All trains from Uppingham had to have a clear run to Seaton, but the signalman accepted a late-running Birmingham to Lowestoft service, resulting in this special leaving Uppingham about twenty minutes late; the goods service ceased from 1 June 1964.

Above: The first railway to arrive at Market Harborough was the LNWR line from Rugby opening in 1850 that was extended towards Luffenham in 1851. In 1857, the MR route from Leicester opened through Market Harborough to Hitchin, and then in 1859, another LNWR line opened to the town from Northampton; this passed through the area of ironstone deposits that came to public attention following the 1851 Great Exhibition. Market Harborough thus became a railway crossroads, and this joint station was opened by the LNWR and MR in 1884. It is May 1958 and we are at the north end of Market Harborough station as a parcels train approaches behind 'Black 5' No. 45253 of Nottingham shed (16A). This locomotive had entered service in 1936 and was one of those built by Armstrong Whitworth rather than by the LMS at Crewe. In 1933, the LMS prepared a scheme for fitting modern Stanier-type boilers to existing classes; there were six boilers proposed and these were sub-divided according to barrel and firebox lengths. The old Highland Railway 'Jones Goods' 4-6-0s dating from the 1890s were even included in this scheme. Later experience suggested that little or no advantage would have accrued from these expensive rebuildings and that Stanier was wise to concentrate on making the case for new locomotives rather than revamping old ones. The 'Black 5s' were thus built in quantity and exceeded all expectations; the first was built in 1934 and by mid-1937, no fewer than 452 were in service.

Opposite page: The Great Northern Railway terminus at Leicester was Belgrave Road, a station not particularly well placed in relation to the city centre. It had seen its first passenger train, an excursion to Skegness, on 2 October 1882, although it was officially opened on 1 January 1883. Leicester Belgrave Road was an imposing terminus with a striking concourse, double-arched roof, and six platforms. The site extended over some 36 acres and included adjoining warehouses and yards. In *The History of the Great Northern Railway 1845-1895* by Charles Grinling, published in 1903, he says the company 'acted with foresight which may yet prove to be enlightened'. Whatever hopes the GNR had never seemed to be fulfilled; in February 1919, there were only three weekday passenger departures. By 1953, just one train each way to Melton Mowbray (two on Saturdays), together with a morning service from John O'Gaunt to Leicester, were dealt with at Belgrave Road, and even these ceased that December. Due to problems with a replacement bus service, the railway was compelled to continue with a workmen's service operated to Leicester from John O'Gaunt only until April 1957, the bus service in turn being withdrawn on 30 September 1963. No. 45238 stands inside Leicester Belgrave Road with the RCTS 'Joint Lines' tour on 18 May 1963, and then outside ready for return to John O'Gaunt.

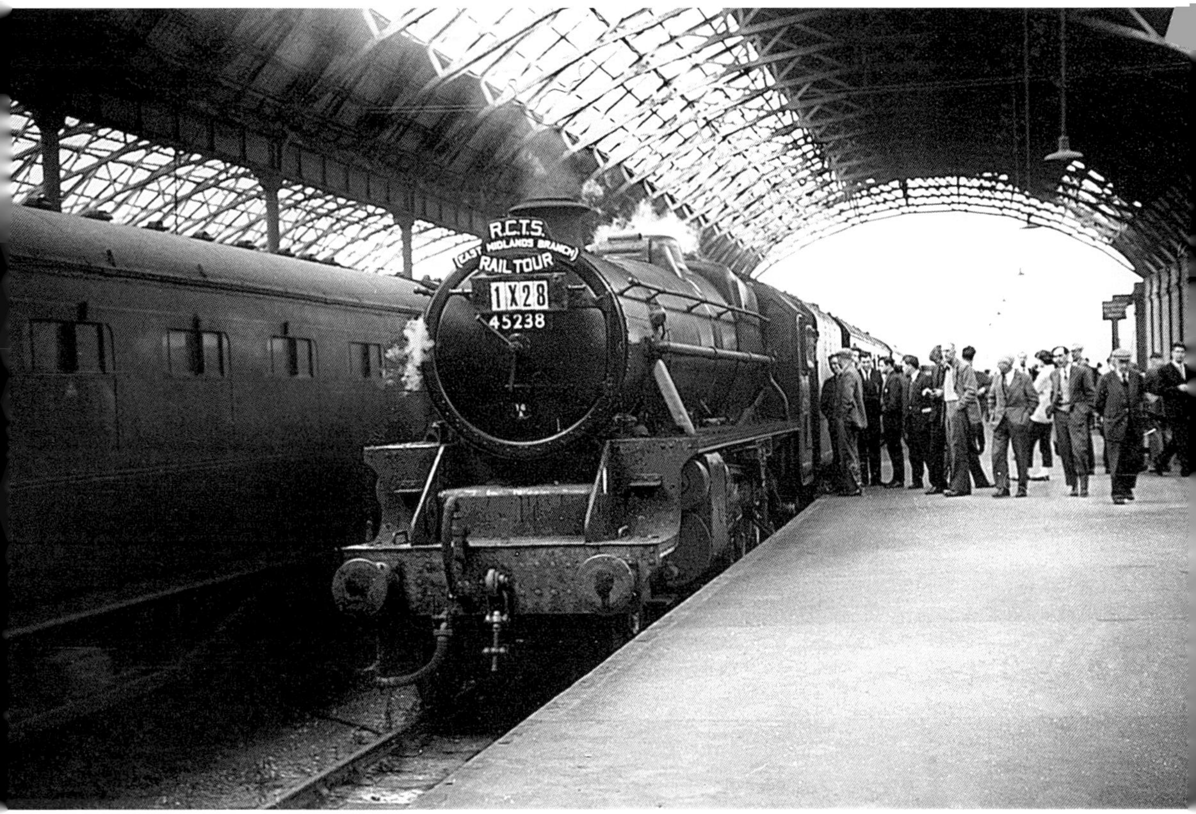
R.C.T.S.
(EAST MIDLANDS BRANCH)
RAIL TOUR
1X28
45238

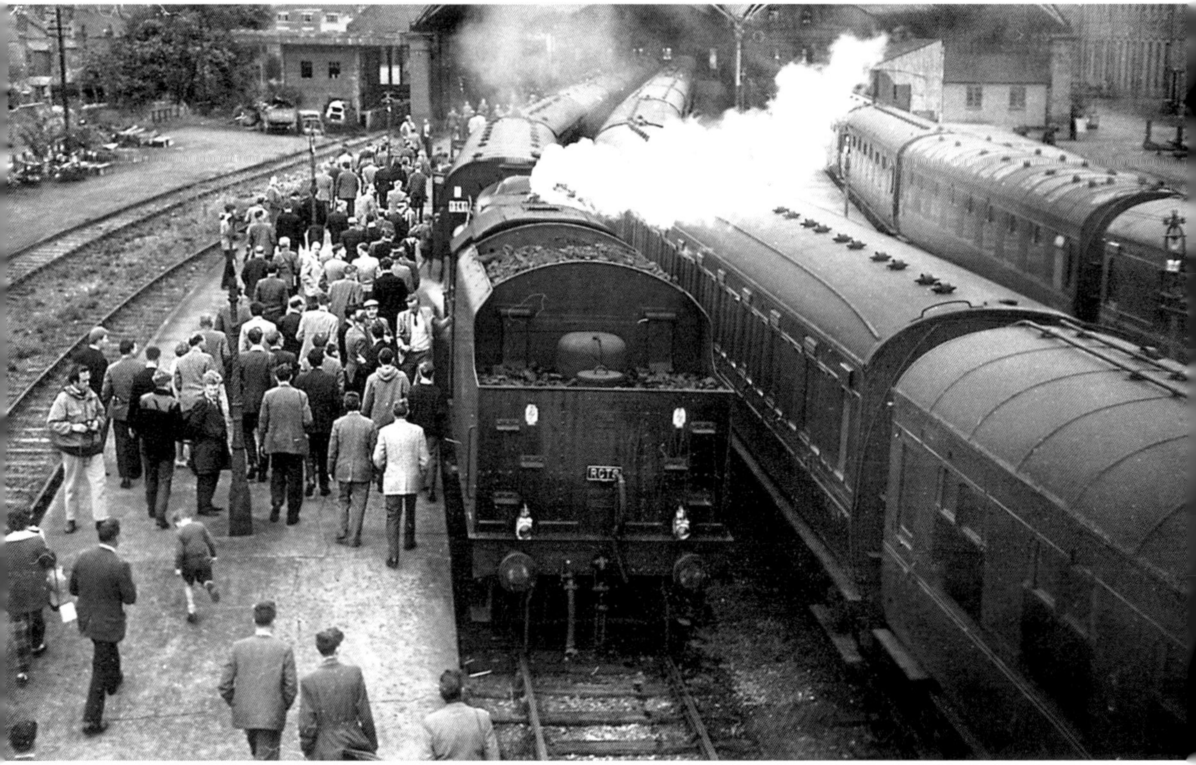
RCTS

Although normal passenger services were withdrawn in the mid-1950s from Leicester Belgrave Road, excursions continued to run during summer months. In 1958, there were forty-eight to Skegness (96.75 miles in about 160 minutes) and twenty-seven to Mablethorpe (102.75 miles in about 180 minutes) with an average of 251 passengers per train. From Leicester Belgrave Road, the line towards John O'Gaunt involved a 5.5-mile climb with grades as steep as 1 in 100 ascending the Leicestershire Wolds. Both photographs date from August 1954: the first is at Humberstone station, 1.5 miles from Belgrave Road, while the second is looking east at Ingarsby (Ingarsby for Houghton according to the station sign) and some 6.5 miles from Leicester. The state of the track became a major concern and the entire distance from Belgrave Road to Marefield Junction had a 25-mph restriction, even so, at Ingarsby and Lowesby engines could still be seen lurching badly. It was the poor state of the track that led to the decision to stop the excursion traffic, these ceasing in September 1961. Freight lasted until 1964 from Marefield Junction, when a spur from the MR main line at Leicester was recommissioned, allowing freight to reach the Catherine Street oil depot nearby Belgrave Road station; total closure came about at the beginning of 1969.

One of the earliest railways in the country was the Leicester and Swannington, which opened in 1832, its prime function being to transport coal from the West Leicestershire coalfield to Leicester; it became the oldest constituent of the Midland Railway. By 1849, a new MR line had been opened between Leicester and Burton-on-Trent that replaced much of the original L&S, but between Desford Junction and Leicester West Bridge was left unchanged and reduced to the status of a branch line. Both photographs were taken on 8 February 1963, firstly Leicester West Bridge station and then No. 58143 shunting the yards north-east of the station (see also page 12); there is still snow on the ground after the bad winter of 1962–63. By the end of the nineteenth century, the passenger service had become three return trains each way, from Leicester West Bridge to Desford. At Desford, connection was made with Leicester London Road to Coalville services that used the 'new' 1849 link. London Road was more centrally placed than West Bridge, and the passenger service came to an end, with the last trains running on Saturday, 22 September 1928; there was never a Sunday service. Substantial freight traffic continued though and West Bridge possessed a large coal yard and a Shell oil depot, and also handled considerable quantities of cement and fertiliser.

Above and opposite page: Three more photographs dating from 8 February 1963, all of them along the Leicester West Bridge to Desford Junction branch and taken on Kodak Ektachrome film. By this time, the motive power was of special interest; the 1870s-built MR Johnson 2F 0-6-0s were the largest permitted on the branch because of the restricted clearance through Glenfield Tunnel. It was about 1 mile in length, perfectly straight and nearly level, but its narrow bore restricted vehicles to a maximum height of 10 feet 9 inches and 7 feet 7 inches in width (according to railway historian C. R. Clinker). One of the very first railway tunnels, it attracted much local interest—an almost irresistible attraction—such that gates and warning boards were erected in 1832 to keep intruders out. The first two views are at Glenfield station with No. 58143 engaging in shunting, coal being the main business here by 1963. The level crossing gates over Station Road had to remain closed to road traffic while shunting. To the left is the original station house, while on the right is the 1876-built station building, the west end of the tunnel being a short distance behind the station (but not visible). The final view is of No. 58143 standing by the signal box at Desford Junction where the branch from West Bridge joined the main route from Leicester to Burton-on-Trent. By the early 1960s, there were two (one on Saturdays) weekday return freight trains over the branch, the locomotive starting from Coalville shed around 4 a.m. and not getting back until about 9 p.m. At the start of 1963, the three 2Fs allocated to Coalville especially for the West Bridge branch were the last survivors of a once numerous class; No. 58143 was built by Dübs of Glasgow in 1875 and had received its last major overhaul in November 1957. Freight continued to Leicester West Bridge from Desford Junction until April 1966, although from December 1963, it was in the hands of two BR Standard Class 2 2-6-0s instead of the old 2Fs; the BR Class 2s were specially modified at Crewe at a cost of £300 apiece to cope with Glenfield Tunnel.

Above and opposite page: It is June 1958 and these three views are all of the LNWR station at Loughborough Derby Road. As a result of negotiations in the mid-1860s, between the LNWR and MR reciprocal arrangements were agreed that would avoid the construction and costs of duplicate railways around the borderland of West Leicestershire in exploiting its coalfields and local industry. A joint railway was built north from Nuneaton that opened in 1873, and the year after an Act was passed for a line from what became Charnwood Forest Junction (near Coalville) on this joint network to Loughborough Derby Road—the Charnwood Forest Railway. The Act provided the railway should be worked for 50 per cent of gross receipts by the LNWR in perpetuity and the single-track line opened throughout in April 1883. However, in 1885, it was adjudged bankrupt and it stayed in receivership until 1909, although the LNWR continued working the line for their 50 per cent and it remained independent until absorption by the LMS at the Grouping. Upon opening, a passenger service of four trains each way daily (except Sundays) was worked from Nuneaton (LNWR) through to Loughborough Derby Road, but from 1890, most trains ran only from Shackerstone, where connection was made with Nuneaton to Ashby services. Passenger services succumbed in April 1931, although freight continued to Loughborough Derby Road until 1955 when it was cut back to Shepshed, and, following this, the line on to Loughborough was used for wagon storage. The first view of the area outside the station includes our family Vauxhall—UWP 701—while the second shows the single (and by now trackless) platform on the right, plus the row of stored wagons on the left that stretch into the distance. These stored wagons apparently attracted criticism from nearby residents who regarded them as an eyesore. The final photograph shows the view in the opposite direction with the single platform now on the left; the keen-eyed may even be able to spot your author (aged six) standing under the station canopy.

Looking east from the road bridge at Saxby station junction and believed taken in July 1962 as a 'Peak' class diesel heads towards Melton Mowbray. This rural part of Leicestershire conceals a complex history. The row of trees to the left of the signal box follows the route of the Oakham Canal that had opened in stages during the early years of the nineteenth century. When the railway from Syston to Peterborough was being considered, a deal was struck with the canal company and it was sold to the MR. The line of the original railway was further to the left and out of sight as it curved through about 90 degrees around a corner of Lord Harborough's Stapleford Park; in fact, the railway experienced many problems with his Lordship and there was even a 'Battle of Saxby'. The original sharp curve was considered unsuitable for the express services between Nottingham and London St Pancras via Manton, so instead, the route the diesel is approaching over was constructed in 1892 with a less severe curve. As the original Saxby station was now bypassed, a new one was built (closed February 1961) on the other side of the road bridge this view is taken from. When all these works were being undertaken, the MR came across what turned out to be an Anglo-Saxon cemetery and very responsibly called in an archaeologist. The next change happened in 1893, when Saxby became a junction with the MR-built connection to the Midland and Great Northern Joint Railway near Little Bytham, Lincolnshire (note the zero milepost by the signal box), and creating a through route to East Anglia. This is the single-track line heading east and to the left of the approaching express. Passenger services over the M&GN had ceased in 1959 and, by 1962, this section was open for freight only to Buckminster Siding, where connection was made with Buckminster Ironstone quarries; this continued until 1966.

Two more photographs from June 1958, but we have moved to Ashby-de-la-Zouch. The station sign is visible in the first view, on the 1849-opened MR line from Burton-on-Trent to Leicester; originally called Ashby, the de-la-Zouch was added in 1924. The track on the station forecourt was that of the Burton and Ashby Light Railway; a section of this rail is still here today. It was a narrow-gauge (3 feet 6 inches) overhead electric tramway and operated from 1906 to 1927, closure coming about due to the success of competing bus services. The second photograph, looking north, shows the remains of Ashby's other station on the line from Derby and Melbourne: this MR route was open throughout by 1874. Passenger services were withdrawn in September 1930 but freight continued; however, shortly after the Second World War started, the line was taken over by the military. Called the Melbourne Military Railway, it was used for training personnel in various aspects of railway operation, and the line from Chellaston East Junction to north of Ashby was handed over to the War Department. It was handed back to the LMS at the beginning of 1945, but closed as a through route in 1955, after which this short section at Ashby remained connecting to local industry.

A railway was first proposed between Ashby and Hinckley in the 'Railway Mania' of the mid-1840s. The MR defeated this projected line by proposing their own, including purchase of the Ashby Canal, which practically paralleled it, but even though they acquired the canal, their proposed line lapsed. As described at Loughborough Derby Road (page 78), in the mid-1870s a railway did come about between Ashby and Nuneaton but it was a joint venture between the MR and LNWR. Stoke Golding was on this joint line, about 4 miles north of Nuneaton, and is seen in the first photograph that dates from February 1961; this view is facing north and taken from the station road bridge. Although passenger services had been withdrawn at Stoke Golding in April 1931, freight continued until August 1962 and wagons are visible in the goods yard. In many ways, it is the view in the second photograph that holds the most intrigue, this is looking in the opposite direction from the same bridge. Curving off to the left can be seen the impression of the one-time line that connected Stoke Golding to Hinckley. This double-track railway was built at the same time as that from Nuneaton to Ashby, but was never used; in the mid-1880s, the signals, junctions, and track were removed, and it remained abandoned thereafter.

On Sunday, 1 March 1959, the Locomotive Club of Great Britain (LCGB) ran a half-day trip of lines around Burton-on-Trent. Departure had been from Derby Midland at 1.15 p.m. behind Burton-allocated Ivatt Class 2 2-6-2T No. 41328, this locomotive having sole charge of the tour, which was just over four hours long. A three-coach push-pull set was used due to the number of reversals, the first of which was at Tutbury, where No. 41328 is taking on water in misty conditions at the west end of the station. Close examination of No. 41328 reveals it has a damaged capuchon (the raised lip at the top of the chimney). From Tutbury, the tour headed for Burton-on-Trent and its maze of railways and sidings, through Rolleston-on-Dove, Stretton Junction, and along the LNWR Horninglow goods-only line that paralleled the Trent and Mersey Canal for 1.75 miles before curving round to Shobnall Junction. The second photograph shows the approach to Wellington Street Junction signal box and its level crossing, while to the right are some of the seemingly infinite number of sidings (especially brewery sidings) that used to exist there. No. 41328 is now on MR tracks, with the left-hand signal in front indicating the special will travel straight on and then underneath the main line from Birmingham to Derby.

Two more views of the LCGB tour around Burton-on-Trent on 1 March 1959. The first photograph shows Dale Street, a typical MR-style signal box. In addition to the road crossing, this box also controlled access to more sidings in the distance, while the line branching at the bottom of the photograph is that to Leicester Junction Sidings (the tour will traverse this in the next commentary). We are on the Bond End branch that had previously been the Bond End Canal; this canal dated from around 1770, was just over a mile long, and connected to the Trent and Mersey Canal via a lock at Shobnall Wharf. By the early 1870s, the canal was more or less derelict, it was filled in for most of its length and had rails laid. The LCGB tour is travelling over these tracks that today are largely converted to roads. In the middle distance of the second photograph is James Street signal box; this box was unusual in having glazing on all four sides and it controlled access to yet more sidings. The tour did not go directly past this box as it is instead on the track that led to Bond End Wharf.

The LCGB tour has now travelled along the Bond End branch as far as it could; the track did continue a little further, but was in a much-neglected state. Behind the wagon by the loading dock is Branston Road Crossing signal box, the crossing gates being for the main A38 road, and further still are the former Peach & Co. Maltings. There were no platforms at Bond End Wharf; instead, tour participants were provided with ladders against the coaches in order to alight (more clearly seen on page 10). The buildings to the right of No. 41328 are those of the Midland Joinery. From Tutbury, the tour has run all the way with the locomotive pulling its three coaches, but this will now alter and, after a scheduled ten-minute stop, No. 41328 will change to push-mode. The view at this spot today bears no resemblance to that on 1 March 1959: a new road bridge has been built over the River Trent from the old Bond Street Wharf, and this area is now under tarmac, with retail and industrial units on either side. The second photograph shows No. 41328 propelling its train up the link between Dale Street Junction and Leicester Junction, the tour is on its way to Woodville Goods Depot via Swadlincote (including another reversal at Woodville Goods Junction).

The next place tour participants were able to stretch their legs on the LCGB tour of 1 March 1959 was the terminus of Woodville Goods (see introductory photograph on page 10). However, this photograph was taken in June 1958 from what was then the A50 road bridge and looking north. This station at Woodville was originally reached in 1850 by an MR branch off the Burton-on-Trent to Leicester line. It used the strange name of Wooden Box until 1868, (the town of Woodville being formerly called Wooden Box after a toll booth on the main road). In 1883, another Woodville station was built on the Swadlincote Loop and this original station became the goods depot for the town. The station building consisted of a two-storey red brick house with its gable at a right angle to the track, plus an amenities block. A peculiarity at Woodville was running round, which was only possible by passing through the timber goods shed to the side of the station building—but apparently this was not permitted. The siding on the right used to extend beyond the station and curve round by 90 degrees to reach the Excelsior Pottery on the far left, which had three bottle kilns. As at Bond End Wharf, there was no platform at Woodville Goods and, in the world before Health and Safety assessments, ladders were used to alight from the LCGB tour; your author (aged seven) has a lasting memory of falling down them and cutting his knee. Freight facilities were withdrawn at Woodville Goods on and from 2 March 1964; nowadays, the station area is an industrial site.

The scheduled departure from Woodville Goods towards Coalville on the 1 March 1959 LCGB trip was 3 p.m.; the first of these photographs shows a part-view of Coalville engine shed taken from the train. This was where the 2F 0-6-0s for the Leicester West Bridge branch were allocated, and on the far side of the turntable is No. 58163, with the old BR symbol on its tender. In January 1959, there were still seventy of this class in service, and although No. 58163 is stored out of use with sacking over its chimney, it remained on the active list for well over two years. The route through Coalville Town station in the second view, looking to the north-west, was that of the Leicester and Swannington Railway and dated from the 1830s. Initially, the station here was known as Long Lane, becoming Coalville in 1848, and Coalville Town in 1924. On Sunday, 1 March 1959, there was an engineering train at the opposite platform to the LCGB tour with 4F No. 43975 attached to the far end. This view is taken from the station footbridge and, out of sight behind it, engineering work was taking place. Passenger services finished at Coalville in September 1964, the station buildings were demolished in 1976, and, although the railway is still in place, it sees little use nowadays.

A final two views of the LCGB tour around Burton-on-Trent and Coalville hauled by No. 41328 on 1 March 1959 that we have been following over the last few pages. From Coalville, the tour traversed the link to Charnwood Forest Junction (to join the one-time route from Loughborough Derby Road) and then went south over the joint MR and LNWR line to Shackerstone, where another reversal took place and the first photograph was taken. This station had opened in 1873, but closed to passengers in April 1931, and ceased to be a junction in 1964 when the line to Charnwood Forest Junction shut. The end came in 1971, when the line from Nuneaton via Shackerstone and on to Moira Junction (on the Burton to Leicester line) closed as a through route. However, the railway at Shackerstone has been born again and is now headquarters of the heritage 'Battlefield Line' that runs to Market Bosworth. The very last photograph of the tour is at Egginton Junction after passing over the Great Northern Railway spur from Dove Junction (north of Burton-on-Trent) to join the still-open-today North Staffordshire Railway route from Uttoxeter towards Derby; ahead in the mist can just be made out Egginton Junction station, which closed in 1962.

The Great Northern Railway established themselves in the Nottingham area during the early 1850s when they took over the Ambergate, Nottingham, Boston and Eastern Junction Railway. This gave the GNR access to Nottinghamshire and its coalfields from Grantham, something the MR had been keen to prevent. The GNR were both physically and legally well-established around Nottingham by the early 1860s and cast envious eyes westwards to the Erewash Valley, at that time the centre of the East Midlands coalfield and an MR monopoly. The MR offered a traffic sharing arrangement that kept the peace for a while, but by 1870, differences came to a head. The GNR's answer was a Bill to serve the coalfields by their own track and more. The new railway ran north of Nottingham, carrying the GNR to the very heart of the MR at Derby and even further by its own tracks plus running powers to Burton-on-Trent and eventually Stafford. Parliamentary blessing was given in June 1872 and some 40 miles of new line were added to the GNR, who could now also attract Derbyshire coal traffic. Such were the GNR's thoughts of expansion in the 1870s that there were even ideas of an alliance with a line whose finances were in a parlous state—the Potteries, Shrewsbury and North Wales Railway (the later Shropshire and Montgomeryshire)—with aspirations of reaching the Welsh coast from London King's Cross, but it came to nothing. Taken on 12 November 1961, the station in this photograph, with a GNR somersault signal, is Etwall. The view is looking south and the station was some 6.5 miles south-west of Derby on the GNR's Derbyshire and Staffordshire Extension. Etwall lost its passenger service in December 1939.

90

Above and opposite page: Although my father died at the relatively young age of sixty-five in 1987, most of his railway friends lived for many years longer. The last survivor of all these old pals—Robert Ellis James-Robertson (but always known as Ellis)—passed away in the spring of 2015 at the age of ninety-two. It was Ellis who very powerfully told me not to give my father's archive to a museum where it may just stagnate, but instead to keep it alive—thus coming about all the videos, books, and film shows I have done over the past twenty-plus years. I like to think that one of the reasons Ellis's daughters contacted me to give a home to their father's railway photographic collection was because of this. It is my wish to also make Ellis's archive come alive, and in future years to hopefully publish a photo-book or perhaps even photo-books in Ellis's name, and I have the blessing of his daughters to do this. As a taster, I have included these three photographs, all of which were taken by Ellis on 29 April 1961, when he travelled on the RCTS 'Vale of Belvoir' rail tour. The first two are at Newark North Gate station, where 9F No. 92177 is hauling a northbound mixed freight that includes ironstone in the first ten or so wagons; according to the tour report, this train backed into the sidings. Tour participants are thronging on the main down platform and giving No. 92177 an admiring glance. This locomotive has a sad claim to fame as it was the first of the 9Fs to be withdrawn in May 1964, in fact one of a batch of seven Eastern Region examples withdrawn at the same time (No. 92223 was withdrawn earlier in February 1964 but was re-instated and survived until 1968). The tour visited a number of ironstone sites, and the third photograph shows *Stanton No. 21*, an Avonside 0-6-0 built in 1901 with a works number of 1424. This was seen at Holwell Ironworks, Asfordby Hill where it attempted to race the tour's DMU. (*R. Ellis James-Robertson*)

Above and opposite page: Although perhaps a rather lowly position in football hierarchy, my father was a Director of Worcester City Football Club from the late 1950s through to the early 1960s. This was the era that Worcester City became known as 'giant-killers' because of beating Liverpool in the FA Cup during January 1959. My father attended some of Worcester's away games during this period, and these three photographs at Sutton Bridge date from the spring of 1960 on his way to a match at King's Lynn, although the precise date was not known. However, according to the King's Lynn FC website, they played Worcester at home in the Southern League Cup on Wednesday, 23 March 1960 (and lost 0–2 to Worcester). The village of Sutton Bridge dates back less than 200 years, and was another that featured in 'Railway Mania' proposals, but had to wait until 1862 for its first line to arrive from Holbeach and the west, built by the Norwich & Spalding Railway. Next was the Lynn & Sutton Bridge Railway, who opened their line from the east in 1864, and for their crossing of the River Nene at Sutton Bridge they used half the width of the 1850-opened road bridge. The final line to arrive was from the south, the Peterborough, Wisbeach (*sic*) & Sutton Bridge Railway in 1866. In 1893, all the three lines became part of the Midland and Great Northern Joint Railway, and after the Grouping, remained jointly owned by the LMS and LNER. The Crosskeys Bridge, visible in all the photographs, was east of the station and built between 1894 and 1897, half for rail traffic and half for road. This third river crossing built at Sutton Bridge is a swing bridge and still swings today, allowing river traffic along the Nene to reach Wisbech. After closure of the railway over the bridge in 1959 and on to South Lynn, the railway section was later converted to road use (a freight service to Sutton Bridge continued until 1965 from the west).

The world speed record for a steam locomotive is 126 mph, which was achieved by *Mallard* descending Stoke Bank between Grantham and Peterborough in 1938; the bank is about ten miles long and mostly at a grade of between 1 in 178 and 1 in 200. Although dieselisation had taken a hold of many regular passenger trains over Stoke Bank by 1962, this was not the case on summer Saturdays, when virtually all the extra services were still steam-hauled, these photographs being taken on Saturday 14 July. A problem was the weather, it was poor to begin with and went downhill during the day. Normally we would move about and film from a variety of locations, but this time refuge was found under the Corby Road bridge close to Swayfield near the top of the bank, and we stopped in the dry. Coming up the bank is A1 No. 60140 *Balmoral*, one of forty-nine constructed after nationalisation. Between December 1961 and May 1963, twenty-one of the class, including No. 60140, had the handrail above the smokebox door hinge replaced by two shorter rails, thus enabling the top lamp iron to be lowered. Coming down the bank, with Dennis Bath also taking a photograph, is A3 No. 60109 *Hermit*—note the higher position of the number plate and top lamp iron, but no split handrail compared to No. 60140.

Another two photographs taken during a visit by my father to King's Lynn for a football match against Worcester City, and, as at Sutton Bridge, the date is believed to be 23 March 1960. The first railways arrived at King's Lynn in the 1840s, but the line through here at South Lynn opened in 1864—the Lynn & Sutton Bridge Railway—although South Lynn station did not open until 1886. Like Sutton Bridge, the passenger service at South Lynn had been withdrawn on and from 2 March 1959, and this view of the derelict island platform is looking west. Looking east, on the right is South Lynn engine shed whose last steam locomotive would be transferred away later that year. The line going straight ahead is the 1 January 1886-opened link line to Bawsey that permitted through-running from Fakenham to Sutton Bridge, avoiding reversal in King's Lynn itself. In the distance, a steam-hauled freight can be seen going from left to right, this is on the still-open line from King's Lynn to Ely. Of the three tracks curving to the left behind South Lynn Junction signal box, the two on the right will join the line from Ely at Harbour Junction, while that on the left connected to the manure works.

Another of our round trips happened on 21 February 1961, this time starting from Northampton Castle over the LNWR line to Peterborough East (the Great Eastern Railway station), using this ticket. However, this photograph is at the city's Great Northern Railway station of Peterborough North and the one still open today (Peterborough East having closed in 1966). The suffixes 'East' and 'North' were added in 1923 after the Grouping, when the LNER found they had two stations in Peterborough. Noticeable is the curve approaching the station, which was subject to a 20 mph speed restriction; it was not until the 1970s that the track layout was altered to provide high speed through lines. Arriving from London King's Cross is the morning down Pullman Car service to Sheffield Victoria and due here at 12.39 p.m., there were two return workings daily for this stock from Monday to Friday. The locomotive is one of the 2,000-hp English Electric Type 4s (later Class 40s); early members featured the white headcode discs for daylight use and also flexible gangway doors, these giving the ability for train crew to move between locomotives when coupled in multiple. Five of these diesels based at Hornsey depot, London, were scheduled to begin working along the East Coast Main Line from Monday, 15 September 1958 (the beginning of the winter timetable). Each locomotive had ten hours overhaul time on one day per week and they were scheduled intensively, typically about 4,500 miles per week.

On 29 August 1844, a headline in *The Times* stated 'Total defeat of the London & York Railway scheme', this coming about following a public meeting at Stamford. The result was that the Great Northern Railway main line from London to the north (authorised on 26 June 1846) passed through Peterborough instead of Stamford. A prosperous town of some 8,000 inhabitants on the Great North Road, Stamford found itself isolated from the railway network by some 4 miles. The decision appears to have been regretted quickly, for although the MR cross country route from Syston (Leicester) to Peterborough was open throughout by 1848 and served Stamford, the lack of a direct link with both London and the north was keenly felt. This seems to have been especially so for the Marquis of Exeter, who lived at Burghley House near Stamford: he had opposed the London to York scheme. As the GNR would not now go to Stamford, Stamford decided instead to go to the GNR, and the leading spirit was the Marquis of Exeter. The Stamford & Essendine Railway Act was passed on 5 August 1853; the line (built for double-track) opened on 1 November 1856 and was worked by the GNR (Essendine being on the GNR main line). The Marquis held the majority of the shares and the line is sometimes referred to as 'The Marquis of Exeter's Railway'. A further development for the Stamford & Essendine Railway was an Act dated 25 July 1864, and this was for a line south from Stamford to join the LNWR route from Northampton to Peterborough at Wansford. This line opened on 9 August 1867, but closed completely on 1 July 1929; it was reported as early as 1906 that it was not unusual for trains to run without passengers. This photograph is of Wansford Road station on the 1929-closed line; it was taken on 29 February 1960, looking towards Stamford.

By the late 1960s, East Midlands ironstone quarrying was in decline and the last system exclusively worked by steam was here at Nassington; it opened in 1939 and was adjacent to the LNWR line from Yarwell Junction, Wansford to Seaton. Two similar Hunslet 0-6-0s worked here: *Jacks Green* (built 1939, W/N 1953) and *Ring Haw* (built 1940, W/N 1982), both names referring to local features. Two visits were made in 1969: the first with snow around the quarry on 13 February in near-ideal photographic conditions, but the second on 11 December, when Eric Parker's diaries refer to the weather as 'wretched all day'. When the LNWR line west of Nassington closed totally in 1968, it provided the opportunity for quarrying to the south of it. The first photograph is in this new quarry with *Jacks Green*, and it was reached from the exchange sidings in the second photograph along the former LNWR trackbed. A new link was then put in from these exchange sidings allowing direct access to the new quarry without reversal, and this is the track behind the wagons coupled to *Ring Haw*. Further behind can be seen a bridge over a now trackless section of the LNWR line, and to the left is the connection to BR at Yarwell Junction. The Nassington system closed at the end of 1970.

Huntingdon's first railway opened from St Ives in 1847, but terminated east of the town. Second was the GNR in 1850 from London whose station was more central, and in 1851, a link was opened between them. Next was the MR from the west, their line from Kettering opening in 1866 together with an agreement for MR trains to work through to Cambridge via St Ives. This station opened in 1883; it was jointly owned, and became Huntingdon East in 1923. These photographs are looking towards St Ives and date from around the end of 1958. There were three platforms: the two tracks in the first photograph were connected to the very close ECML, while the third on the other side of the island was for MR services. Note the check rails on the sharp curves and also the safety trap point. Beyond is the closed engine shed, while between the shed and station was the Stationmaster's house. In the summer of 1958, there were three passenger trains daily (except Sundays) between Kettering and Cambridge, plus one extra on Saturdays (a through train each way between Leicester and Clacton). The passenger service ceased in June 1959 and freight in 1962; today, much of this site is part of the car park for Huntingdon's remaining station on the ECML.

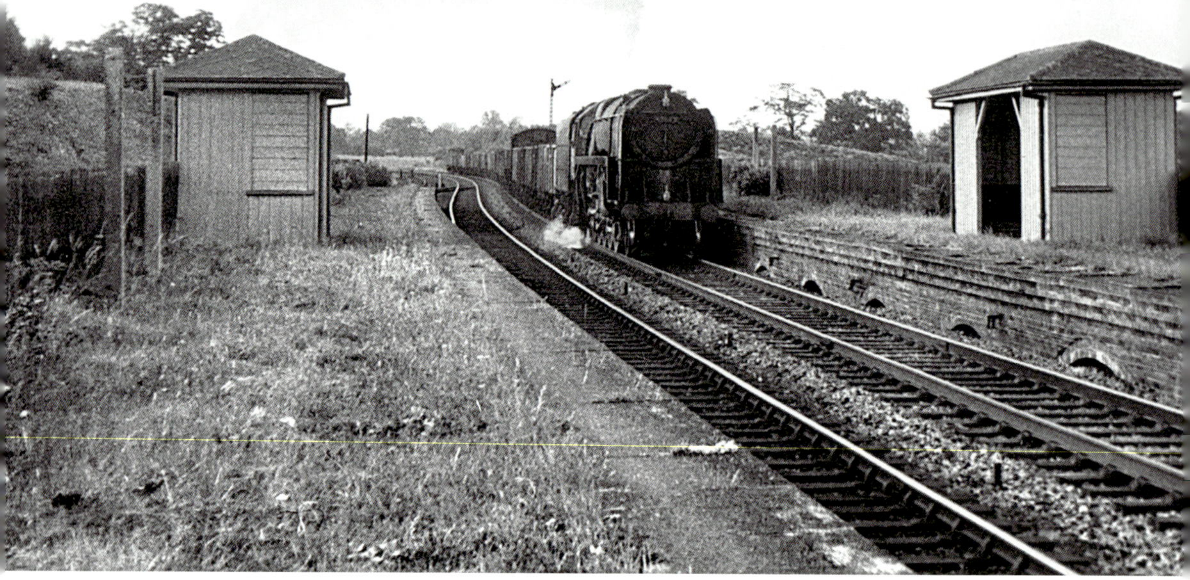

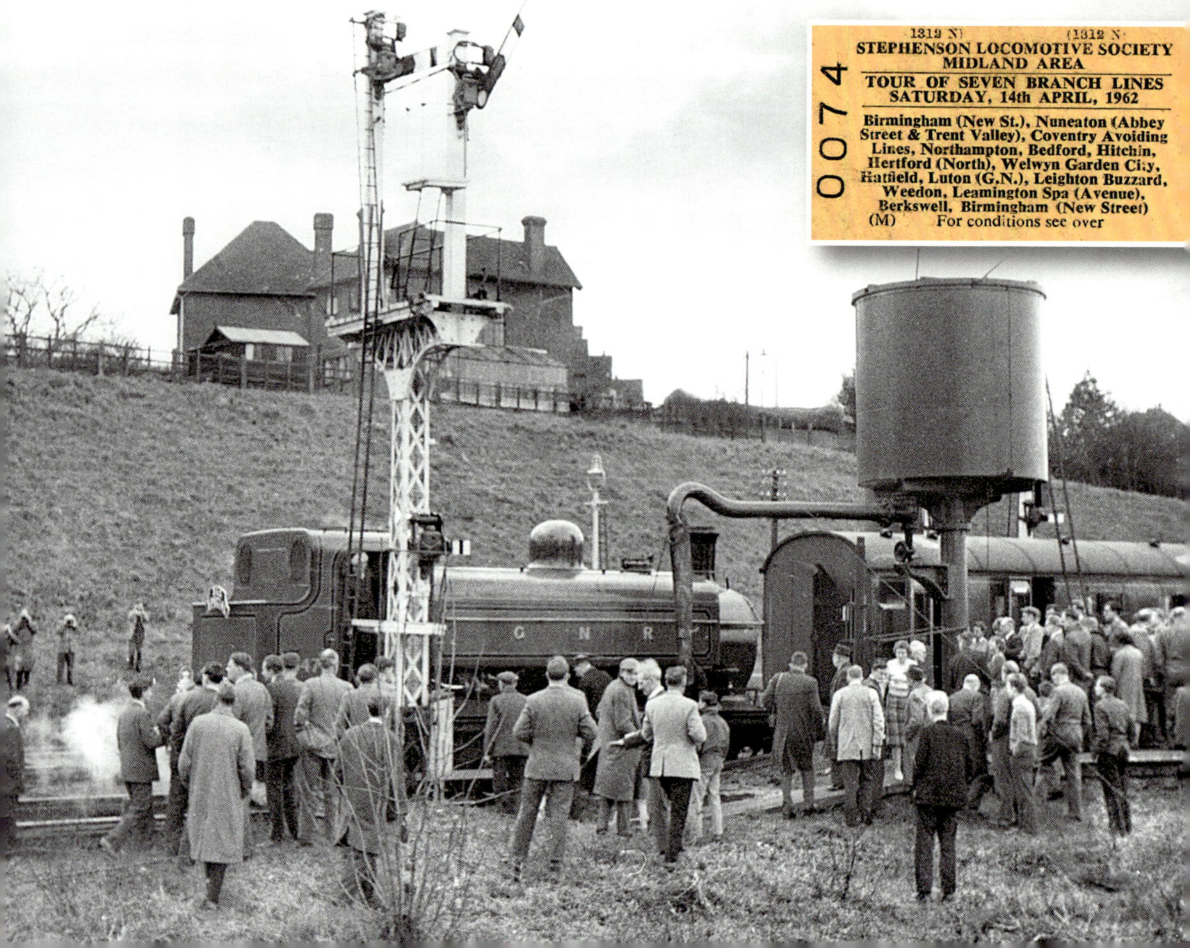
1312 N) (1312 N
STEPHENSON LOCOMOTIVE SOCIETY
MIDLAND AREA
TOUR OF SEVEN BRANCH LINES
SATURDAY, 14th APRIL, 1962
Birmingham (New St.), Nuneaton (Abbey Street & Trent Valley), Coventry Avoiding Lines, Northampton, Bedford, Hitchin, Hertford (North), Welwyn Garden City, Hatfield, Luton (G.N.), Leighton Buzzard, Weedon, Leamington Spa (Avenue), Berkswell, Birmingham (New Street)
(M) For conditions see over
0074
G N R

Above, below, and opposite page: As our journey up the old Great Northern Railway from Peterborough towards London King's Cross reaches Stevenage, the railway splits. The original 1850-opened line onwards through Welwyn is joined by a parallel route branching off the ECML at Langley Junction, Stevenage; this runs east of the main line through Hertford and on to King's Cross, and is known as the Hertford Loop. At the end of the nineteenth century, GNR management were becoming concerned over the two two-track bottlenecks on their main line: firstly, between Greenwood signal box, New Barnet and Potters Bar, and secondly, the area around Welwyn Viaduct; estimates were obtained to widen the lines. As an alternative, a plan was drawn up that would not only bypass the main line bottlenecks, but also open up an area not yet served by the railway with the prospect of new traffic. The plan was to extend the Enfield branch through Cuffley and Hertford North to rejoin the main line at Langley Junction, and contracts were let in 1906 for the new line instead of the widening. Cuffley was reached in 1910, and although completed by 1918, it took until 1924 before double-track was laid and a passenger service started north of Cuffley (as a result, this line is missing from the map on page 7). North of the 1924-opened Hertford North, the passenger service was not a success and it was withdrawn in September 1939; the first two photographs are at one of these closed stations—Stapleford—and thought to date from about 1959. One of the purposes of the Hertford Loop was to divert slow-moving freights away from the main line bottlenecks and a southbound goods train is passing through Stapleford. Today, the line through Stapleford has been electrified and the other closed station north of Hertford—Watton-at-Stone—has been reopened. The third photograph is another of the SLS 'Tour of Seven Branch Lines' special train on 14 April 1962, this time at Hertford North. Hauling the tour is privately preserved Class J52 0-6-0 No. 1247; it has just arrived from Hitchin and will soon depart to Welwyn Garden City and Hatfield.

By the date of this photograph, 8 October 1961, the ECML bottlenecks on the exit from London had been reduced to one. The section between Greenwood signal box, New Barnet, and Potters Bar had by now been quadrupled; it was included in the BR modernisation plans for 1956–57 and involved three new tunnels with an estimated cost of some £2.75 million. The remaining two-track section was from Digswell Junction (north of Welwyn Garden City), over Digswell Viaduct (also called Welwyn Viaduct), through Welwyn North station, then both Welwyn South and North Tunnels to Woolmer Green Junction, a distance of about 2.5 miles. The train being hauled by No. 60021 *Wild Swan* is the Sunday 10.25 a.m. restaurant car express from London King's Cross to Hull, Leeds, and Bradford. On the far left is my father, taking cine film with his camera on a tripod, and his cousin. The train has left the four-track section north of Welwyn Garden City station and is about to pass over the around 1,560-feet-long Digswell Viaduct. This double-track bottleneck is still with us today, as presumably the costs of widening this very difficult section of track outweigh the operational gains; current thoughts seem to centre on a more advanced signalling system to alleviate the problem rather than building extra tracks.

Over three years earlier, in the spring of 1958, we are now on the other side of Digswell Viaduct. This is Welwyn North station, where celebrity A4 No. 60022 *Mallard* is arriving on a southbound service. The station dates from 1850 and was originally just Welwyn, the North being added in 1926 to differentiate it from the present Welwyn Garden City station, which opened that year. Note the difference in the head lamp codes between the previous photograph and this one; one above each buffer with No. 60021 signifies an express passenger train, while No. 60022 here has just a single lamp above its number plate, signifying an ordinary passenger train. There used to be sidings at both ends of the station, and at the north end on the left-hand side, a number of wagons are visible. Today, the sidings at both ends have been largely converted to car parking space. This is a very cramped location; behind the train, Welwyn South Tunnel can just be seen, while a short distance after leaving Welwyn North, No. 60022 will pass over Digswell Viaduct. Nowadays, the standard stopping pattern at Welwyn North is two services in both directions each hour, and fitting these in with non-stop high-speed services is a headache for timetable planners on this double-track section.

Of course, No. 60022 *Mallard* is holder of the world speed record for a steam locomotive—but it may be broken in the future. The University of Minnesota have developed a fuel called 'Torrefied Biomass' as a means to use that state's massive timber reserves (and, importantly in today's world, a sustainable resource). It has similar energy, density, and material handling properties to coal, but without the associated carbon footprint, heavy metal, or sulphur content. The Coalition for Sustainable Rail hope to convert Atchison, Topeka & Santa Fe Railway 4-6-4 No. 3463 to burn this fuel and also add numerous improvements. A similar late 1930s 4-6-4 locomotive in the USA (Chicago, Milwaukee, St Paul & Pacific Railroad) averaged 120 mph for 5 miles with a peak of about 125 mph well over seventy years ago.

Above and opposite: The GNR's original and temporary terminus in London opened in 1850 at Maiden Lane, and it was not until 1852 that King's Cross, the station we generally think of as the GNR's terminus, opened. The sign on the signal box clearly does not have an apostrophe, yet the BR timetables (from 1959 to 1962) in front of me as I write this do. Both photographs were taken on Thursday, 26 October 1961: in the first, A3 No. 60109 *Hermit* is at the north end of the station waiting to depart, with the fireman inspecting the coal in the tender; we have seen this locomotive previously on Stoke Bank in July 1962 (page 94). It was one of the earlier class members entering service in July 1923, yet had a double chimney fitted in March 1959 and the trough-style smoke deflectors added in January 1961. *Hermit* was withdrawn in December 1962. At the other end of the station is A4 No. 60030 *Golden Fleece*. The first four of this class followed a 'Silver' theme with their names, after which the next intention was to use the names of birds noted for swift and/or powerful flight—*Golden Fleece* was originally named *Great Snipe*, but only for about one month in 1937; No. 60030 was also withdrawn in December 1962.

GUIDE AND NOTES TO...
THE JUBILEE REQUIEM
...RAILTOUR

LONDON (KINGS CROSS) — NEWCASTLE (CENTRAL) & BACK

SATURDAY, 24th OCTOBER, 1964

Commemorative Special Train hauled by an
ex-L.N.E.R. Class A4 Pacific Locomotive

Photo: M. W. Earley

THE RAILWAY CORRESPONDENCE AND TRAVEL SOCIETY
and
THE STEPHENSON LOCOMOTIVE SOCIETY
Joint Committee

Above and opposite page: Gresley's streamlined A4 4-6-2s were associated with the ECML expresses from their introduction in 1935 until steam came to an end at King's Cross on Sunday, 16 June 1963, although the very last scheduled steam departure was behind A1 No. 60158 *Aberdonian*, hauling the 10.45 p.m. to Leeds. New England shed, Peterborough, became home for King's Cross top shed's eleven A4s still in service after this; they did appear in the capital deputising for failed diesels until October 1963, after which, following withdrawals and transfers to Scotland, *The Railway Observer* could report that 'for the first time in twenty-eight years the GNR main line is without A4s'. One last special train was organised (with no child tickets), and specifically advertised as 'the last occasion on which an A4 will be allowed to work into or out of King's Cross'. The 'Jubilee Requiem' rail tour took place on Saturday, 24 October 1964 and used A4 No. 60009 *Union of South Africa*, at the time allocated over 500 miles away at Aberdeen Ferryhill shed. The photograph shows the scene at King's Cross before departure to Newcastle scheduled for 7.55 a.m., and not long after sunrise. On the return, No. 60009's speedometer showed 100 mph coming down Stoke Bank, and arrival back at King's Cross was twenty-six minutes early.

Above and opposite page: The Great Central Railway's origins go back to 1847 when, as a result of amalgamations, the Manchester, Sheffield and Lincolnshire Railway was formed. The Great Central name came about fifty years later, not as a result of further mergers, but to herald the opening of its London Extension to Marylebone. What had been a cross-country line achieved trunk line status—Britain's last main line of the Victorian era to London (and the last until High Speed 1 connected the capital to the Channel Tunnel). The London Extension was formally opened here at London Marylebone on 9 March 1899, and passenger trains began six days later. Management had high hopes for the passenger traffic and promoted it with the slogan 'Every express train vestibuled with buffet car attached'. The crack express was the 'Sheffield Special' that once ran with a schedule of two hours and fifty minutes, and in 1905 the GCR ran ten expresses from Marylebone to Sheffield. The diesel-hauled Pullman express we saw over fifty years later at Peterborough in 1961 (page 96) took only five minutes less on its evening run from London to Sheffield, with one stop. However, by the time of these photographs on 31 March 1966 (the date of the ticket), with 'Black 5' No. 44984 preparing to depart for Nottingham Victoria, Marylebone and the London Extension were in seemingly terminal decline, and the Nottingham line would in fact close as a through route in the September. A closure notice for London Marylebone station itself was issued in the 1980s for the remaining services to Aylesbury and the Banbury route. However, such has been the recovery under Chris Green's Network SouthEast, and then following privatisation, with Adrian Shooter, that today, Marylebone station has become a thriving and expanding London terminus.

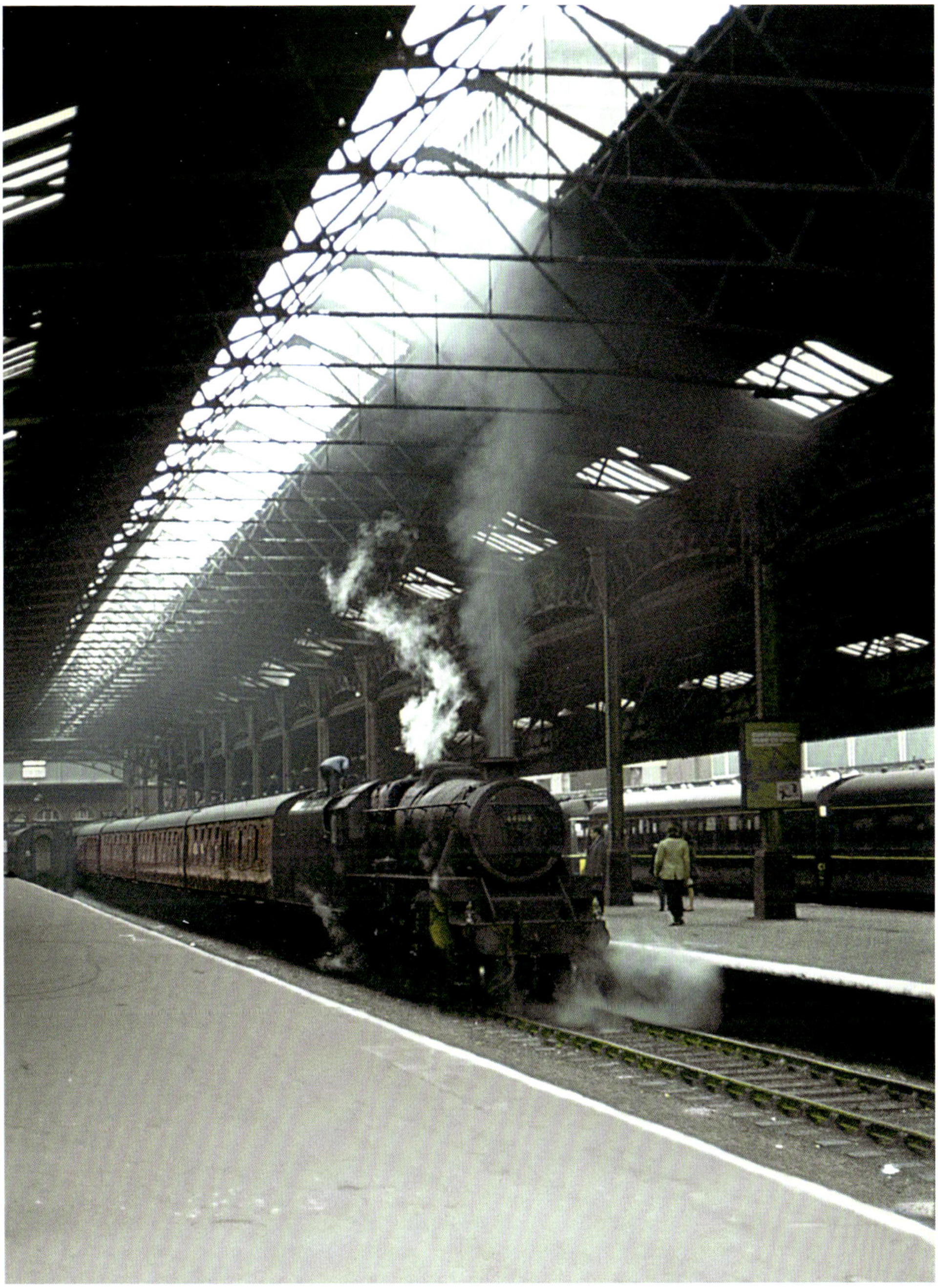

4101
2nd DAY EXCURSION
London (Marylebone) to WOODFORD HALSE
(M) Fare
For conditions see over
DAY EXCURSION 2nd
Woodford Halse to LONDON (Marylebone)
Fare 16/6 (M)
For conditions see over
4101

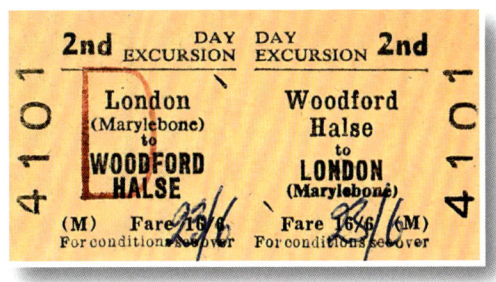

Above and opposite page: It is still 31 March 1966, and 'Black 5' No. 44984, seen previously at Marylebone, has now moved on to Aylesbury Town. Latterly, GC steam-hauled passenger services were operated from Colwick shed at Nottingham, and there were only basic facilities available at the London end, such as water and a turntable. Water could also be topped up at some of the intermediate stations but coal could not be anywhere, thus it was vital that all locomotives on the over 250 miles round trip to London started with their tenders well stacked up with coal. Locomotive problems could also present difficulty, and an example was quoted in the January 1966 edition of *The Railway Observer*. On arrival at Marylebone, the steam engine was found to have defective brakes and a replacement was sought, but D5089 was refused by the guard as it had no steam heating, plus the driver was unable to drive diesels. No replacement steam locomotive could be found, so the service had to wait until the next departure to the north from Marylebone, and the two were combined together. Aylesbury was visited again on 11 August 1966 (the date of the ticket) and by the old GWR engine shed (closed June 1962) was 9F No. 92227. This had replaced a defective 'Black 5' at Culworth Junction but failed itself, and was taken off at Aylesbury.

2nd · SINGLE
Aylesbury to
Lutterworth
via
For alternative routes see book of routes
(M) For conditions see over Fare 14/6
4078 4078

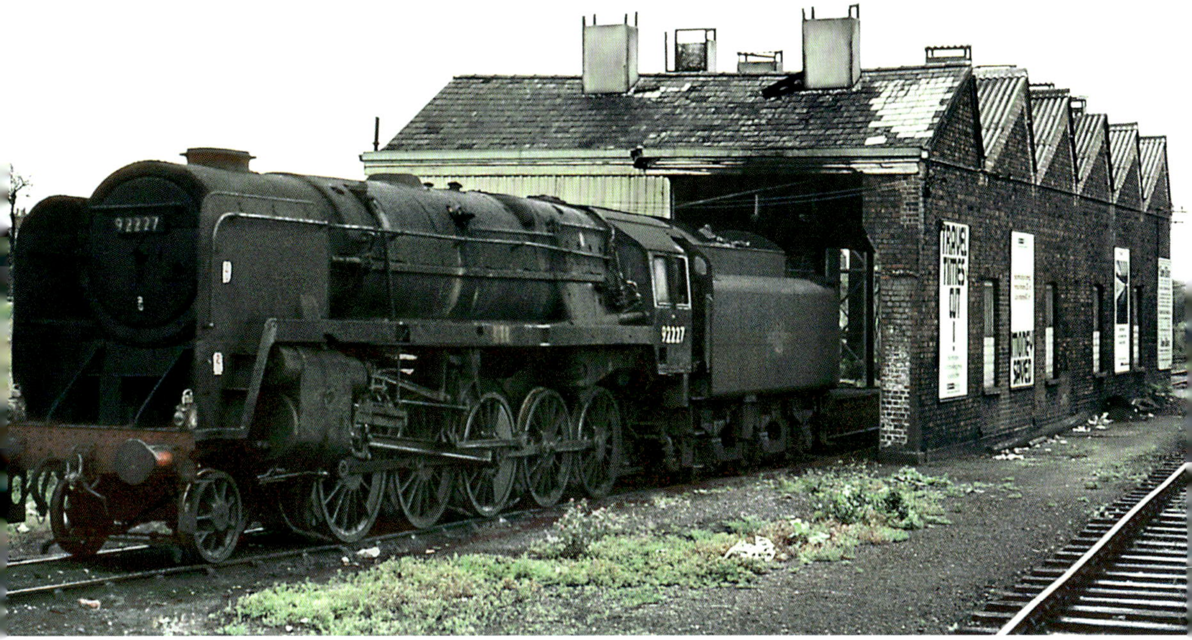

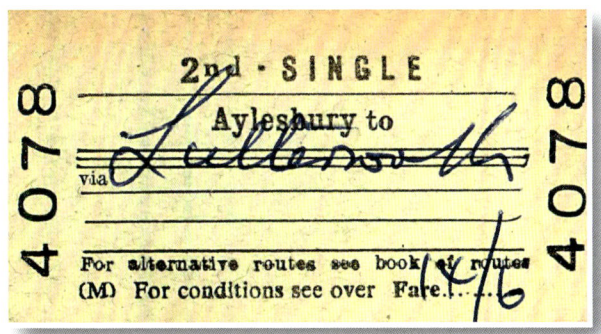

Another visit to Aylesbury Town was made using this return Woodford Halse ticket on Saturday, 9 July 1966. By this time, the days of ten expresses from Marylebone to Sheffield were long-gone, the axe falling at the beginning of January 1960 when all through expresses to Sheffield, Manchester, and Bradford were withdrawn (except a night service). The Sunday passenger service finished in 1963, as did the most of the local stopping trains at the more rural stations. By 1964, the passenger service south of Nottingham consisted of three semi-fasts in each direction between Marylebone and Nottingham Victoria, with connections from the Banbury line at Woodford Halse; a single York to Bournemouth express; and certain local trains between Rugby and Nottingham, plus a variety of overnight trains and holiday extras. It was said at the time 'It is hard to see how the present timetable can really be expected to attract traffic'. From early 1963, steam at Aylesbury Town was reduced further as the 8.38 a.m. from London and 12.30 p.m. return from Nottingham were handed over to a Marylebone four-car suburban DMU set. Many of the steam passenger workings were quite short formations, but an exception was the train in the photograph hauled by 'Black 5' No. 44941. It is the 5.15 p.m. service from Nottingham to Marylebone and will soon depart from Aylesbury on this pleasant summer's evening. The sound of No. 44941's actual departure can be listened to on the author's website in the Sound Bites section of michaelclemensrailways.co.uk.

The Great Central's London Extension ran from Annesley (between Nottingham and Chesterfield) to here at Quainton Road, around 6 miles north of Aylesbury; it was about 92 miles long. Much of the expansion and development of the precursor to the GCR was due to Edward Watkin, who became General Manager of the MS&L in 1854, chairman in 1864, and accepted chairmanship of the Metropolitan Railway in 1872. The existing Metropolitan Railway line from London to Verney Junction (page 36) was joined at Quainton Road. The station in this view opened in November 1896 and is seen on 8 October 1961 looking towards Aylesbury Town; the original station had been behind the photographer, and was described as one of the most primitive-looking in the British Isles. The physical junction of the GC and Metropolitan tracks was a short distance still further behind. The track branching off to the right with its own platform is that of the one-time Brill Tramway, the first section of which opened in 1871; the Metropolitan took over all its operations in December 1899 but closed the line in November 1935. By the date of this photograph, the line to Verney Junction was also closed, but local services along the GCR London Extension still called until they too ceased in March 1963. Today, Quainton Road is headquarters of the heritage Buckingham Railway Centre, and a single-track freight-only line still passes through. Hopefully, if the reopening of the East-West rail link from Oxford to Cambridge continues according to plan, it is proposed to run a service from Aylesbury to Milton Keynes along the track here, and linking to the line from Oxford and Bicester at Claydon Junction.

The MS&L obtained the Act for their London Extension in 1893 and, due its construction at the end of the Victorian era, were able to take advantage of technology that did not exist decades earlier, such as steam excavators. There was significant engineering to allow the relatively easy maximum grade of 1 in 176 as far as Nottingham from Quainton Road and there were no very sharp curves. Being so late in the day, most places already had a service to London, but building a high-speed line was seen as a way to attract traffic. As Edward Watkin (Sir Edward from 1868) had aspirations of reaching Europe through a Channel Tunnel, the line was also built to the larger continental loading gauge. Most stations were island platforms as here at Brackley Central, seen in the summer of 1966 not long before closure. Very often the entrance to stations on the London Extension were from the road bridge (and here the A43 at the north end of the station), but at Brackley Central, following concerns over traffic congestion, a brick booking hall and offices were provided in a lay-by off the main road. Connecting to the platform was this substantial covered footbridge that spanned the down line; Brackley was the only station on the extension built like this.

Two more photographs taken at Brackley Central, the first shows a train already seen at Aylesbury Town—'Black 5' No. 44941 on the 5.15 p.m. from Nottingham Victoria to London Marylebone on Saturday, 9 July 1966; water was available at both ends of the station. The second was taken on 21 July 1966: 'Black 5' No. 44920 is awaiting custom at just after 6 p.m., before heading to the next stop at Woodford Halse with the 4.38 p.m. departure from Marylebone. Note the contemporary chalking on the smoke box door; it reads 'Mod Girls For Ever'. This relatively expensive ticket (not a cheap day return) was issued on Sunday, 17 February 1963, just before withdrawal of Sunday passenger services in the March. In late 1964, proposals for closure of much of the GC's London Extension were published, the most important regarding passenger services being the withdrawal of the London Marylebone to Nottingham semi-fasts. The Marylebone to Aylesbury suburban service was not affected, but the line from Calvert Junction and through Brackley Central to Rugby Central was proposed for total closure. A passenger survey had been carried out in 1964, when it was found the only passengers travelling the entire distance from London to Nottingham or *vice versa* were railway enthusiasts.

The Great Central's London Extension was seen as a high-speed passenger route south from Nottingham and built accordingly. It did serve some centres of population such as Loughborough and Leicester, but south of Rugby the 45 miles or so onwards to Aylesbury traversed a very rural area; even Brackley had a population of only 2,467 in 1901. Nevertheless, some rural stations were opened and these two photographs are at Helmdon for Sulgrave, about 3 miles north of Brackley Central. Even today the village of Helmdon has a population of less than 1,000, plus it was also served by another company's railway station. The even smaller village of Sulgrave is famous for its Manor, the ancestral home of the Washington family (George Washington, President of the USA). The first Helmdon station was on the 1872-opened line between Towcester and Banbury that eventually became part of the SMJR; this line became very useful for bringing in materials for building the later GCR. The GCR's Helmdon Viaduct passed directly over the SMJR route and the navvies created a camp underneath the viaduct. Both photographs were taken on Thursday, 28 February 1963 and just before closure of Helmdon for Sulgrave (plus many of the more rural GCR stations) over that coming weekend, although freight traffic continued here for another eighteen months or so.

A feature of the GC main line south of Nottingham was that while it crossed several other railways, it had few junctions with them. This is Culworth Junction, to the south of Woodford Halse, and seen on Thursday, 1 September 1966, just before total closure in a few days. Behind us is the main line to the north, in front and curving sharply to the right is the 1900-opened double-track connection to the GWR at Banbury, while the route to Brackley Central and Marylebone carries straight on before curving to the right in the distance. From opening in 1899 until the First World War probably represented the GC's nearest approach to the fulfilment of its promoters' ambitions, with the London to Manchester passenger service being its backbone. However, long-distance passenger trains did travel over the link to Banbury and onwards: the diesel-hauled York to Bournemouth cross-country service still went this way, handing over to steam at Banbury for its journey on to the coast. This well-loaded train survived the GC closure by being diverted initially via Derby, Birmingham, and Worcester to reach Oxford. Possibly most intriguing used to be the one-time 'Ports to Ports' express from the north-east to South Wales and very useful for seamen. By the 1930s, this was a restaurant car train from Newcastle-on-Tyne to Cardiff, Barry, and Swansea; it even included a conditional stop at Chipping Norton. By 1960, and with changed traffic patterns, it was said the main line was now that to Banbury, whereas the railway to Marylebone could be considered a branch. The GC had become primarily a trunk route from the north to the west of England, and it was predominately made up of freight traffic.

Certain 'railway towns' are well-known, such as Crewe and Swindon, but another example, nowhere near as large or well-known, was created in a remote corner of west Northamptonshire: Woodford Halse. It was about halfway between Nottingham and London, with plenty of room for railway infrastructure; there was a junction with the already existing East and West Junction Railway (SMJR from 1909), while a little to the south was Culworth Junction and the line to Banbury. This view from the footbridge at Woodford Halse station (Woodford and Hinton until 1948) was taken on Saturday, 9 July 1966, having just arrived from Aylesbury Town behind No. 45292. The station is again the island layout favoured by the GCR, but, unlike at Brackley and Helmdon, the station here was built on an embankment; the passengers on the right are about to descend steps to road level. The terraced houses on the extreme right (they still exist today) were built by the GCR for their staff and families. Ahead on both sides were once massive marshalling yards and also an engine shed complex on the right in the distance. On weekdays in 1960, the yards at Woodford Halse dealt with forty-four northbound arrivals and forty-three northbound departures, while for the south there were forty-two arrivals and forty-seven departures (of which fifteen ran to or from the Brackley direction). Controlling everything were four signal boxes, thirty-three down sidings, eleven up sidings for Banbury, and ten for other destinations. However, the goods traffic was ultimately transferred to other routes, and the last official full day of freight working at Woodford Halse was 11 June 1965 (although the yards seemed all but empty when my father visited on 24 April 1965).

Although from the beginning of 1960 the daytime expresses from Marylebone were withdrawn and the passenger service downgraded, the line was used by other passenger trains, especially so during the summer. The 'Starlight Specials' were cheap period returns between London and Scotland; initially the Marylebone trains ran to Edinburgh Waverley via York, while Glasgow was served from St Pancras, but after the GC became part of the LMR virtually all ran to and from Marylebone. On Friday, 15 July 1960—the first weekend of the Glasgow Fair Holiday— no fewer than twelve 'Starlight Specials' ran to Marylebone: seven from Glasgow St Enoch, two from Edinburgh Waverley, and one each from Kirkcaldy, Cardenden, and Coatbridge. The interchange to and from the GC was achieved by the network of lines north of Nottingham. Then there were three 'Car-Sleeper' trains: to Glasgow St Enoch, Perth, and a Dover to Newcastle service working via Banbury, all of these running only on two or three days a week. However, the 'Starlight Specials' were withdrawn plus the other services were transferred away or ceased. The colour photograph shows No. 45292 at Woodford Halse after arrival from Aylesbury on 9 July 1966 and the second, No. 44847 heading for Aylesbury on 26 May 1966; all the signals are removed and within a few months, everything would be closed down.

The first railway in the Woodford Halse area was the 1873-opened East and West Junction Railway between Stratford-upon-Avon and Towcester, this later becoming part of the SMJR. This is the view looking south-east at Woodford West Junction in about 1960 with the line to Towcester heading into the distance and curving slightly to the left. Curving sharply to the left is the double-track connection opened in 1899 to Woodford and Hinton station (Woodford Halse from 1948). Beyond the signal box, the South Junction line diverged to the right; also opened in 1899, this allowed through-running from London to Stratford-upon-Avon via the GCR but was taken out of use in 1900. Stratford was one of the few towns that the GCR could offer the shortest route to London of any railway company—93.25 miles via Woodford and Aylesbury to Marylebone. The distance by the GWR was 102.75 miles to Paddington via Hatton and Bicester or 110.75 miles via Honeybourne and Oxford. Another alternative was SMJR all the way to Blisworth and then LNWR to Euston (1.75 miles shorter than the GWR via Bicester). With the direct link from here towards Woodford South Junction only used as a siding after 1900, a through service was instead provided by the GCR via Woodford and Hinton station. In July 1904, the GCR offered a fastest time to Stratford of two hours and five minutes, and only marginally slower than today's fastest service by Chiltern Railways. The (by then single) daily through carriage to Stratford was withdrawn on 1 February 1936, this simultaneously also meaning the end of slip-coaches on the route from Marylebone; the same train used to slip at both Finmere and Woodford and Hinton.

When the East and West Junction Railway (later SMJR) opened their line from Towcester to Stratford-upon-Avon in 1873, they did not have a station at Woodford, but they did open one about 2 miles away here at Byfield. Although undated, this view of the station looking towards Woodford West Junction is believed to date from the summer of 1965 and after the line had closed. Goods traffic was the most important on the line; in fact, the passenger service from Towcester through Byfield and on to Stratford had been suspended between 1877 and 1885. The large water tank at the far end of the platform originally used a donkey plodding round in a circle harnessed to a pole to pump the water. Later a stationary steam engine was used that also supplied electricity to light the station, the first so lit on the SMJR. There were also ironstone quarries at Byfield that connected to the SMJR about half-a-mile west of the station. At the 1915-opened exchange sidings on 26 October 1961 in the second photograph is 0-6-0 *Cherwell*, built by Bagnall's of Stafford in 1942 (W/N 2654). The official closure date of the quarry system was July 1965, although the last revenue earning traffic seems to have been in the February; the old SMJR closed through Byfield at the same time.

There was only one ironstone system that connected directly to the GCR's London Extension and it did so in the goods yard of Charwelton station. The Charwelton Quarries system opened in May 1917 and operated until June 1933, when production ceased. It lay dormant until May 1941 when the quarries opened up again due to wartime demands. Another dormant period followed from October 1945 until May 1951 when it reopened yet again. Nominally, the owners were the Park Gate Iron & Steel Company Ltd. of Rotherham, but latterly the system was run jointly with the Staveley Iron & Chemical Company Ltd. By 1960 output was diminishing, with only a single locomotive in use at any one time, and, even though a new quarry was opened up in 1961, the system closed on 18 November 1961 for 'an unknown duration'. No. 8, a Yorkshire Engine Company product built in 1904 (W/N 784), is seen at work on 26 October 1961, less than a month before closure. Whereas *Cherwell* at Byfield in the previous photograph survived to be preserved, No. 8 did not. Track lifting commenced in June 1963 and the delightful No. 8 was cut up on the spot; by the December, it had been reduced to a pile of scrap. Apparently, that well-known enthusiast the Reverend Teddy Boston hoped to buy No. 8, but he arrived too late and cutting up had already started.

Despite Northampton having neither mountains nor a recognised range of hills (such as the Malverns), there is a broken ridge of high ground reaching across from the northern Cotswolds towards the Corby area. As far as railways were concerned, ten tunnels eventually penetrated this high ground, with three being over one mile long. The tunnel we are concerned with here was the last built and also the longest: Catesby Tunnel. The GC's London Extension largely avoided tunnels after clearing Nottingham on its journey south, Catesby being the main exception and second longest on the entire system after Woodhead Tunnel under the Pennines. Catesby Tunnel is north of Charwelton station, and about 10 miles south of Rugby; it is driven beneath Arbury Hill which rises to 738 feet (the highest point in Northamptonshire). The first railway tunnel through this high ground of the county was at Kilsby on the London and Birmingham Railway. Kilsby Tunnel defied the excavators and the original contractor gave up; it cost three times the budget, took an age to complete, and its maintenance headaches continued for decades and decades. However, with Catesby Tunnel being constructed so late in the Victorian era, much experience had been gained in tunnelling, and equipment unknown in the 1830s was to hand. Construction began in February 1895, and it was finished by late May 1897, this year being cut into stone above the tunnel's portal. No major difficulties arose, it encountered little water, and was cut through lower and middle lias. The tunnel is 3,000 yards long, dead straight, and on a rising grade from the north of 1 in 176. Nine shafts were dug during construction, but only five were kept for ventilation, one being visible in this photograph at the Charwelton end and believed taken during the winter following closure in September 1966. As this book is being written, Catesby Tunnel looks to be embarking on a new career, and certainly not one envisaged by the GCR—it is to be converted into an aerodynamic research facility for motor vehicles.

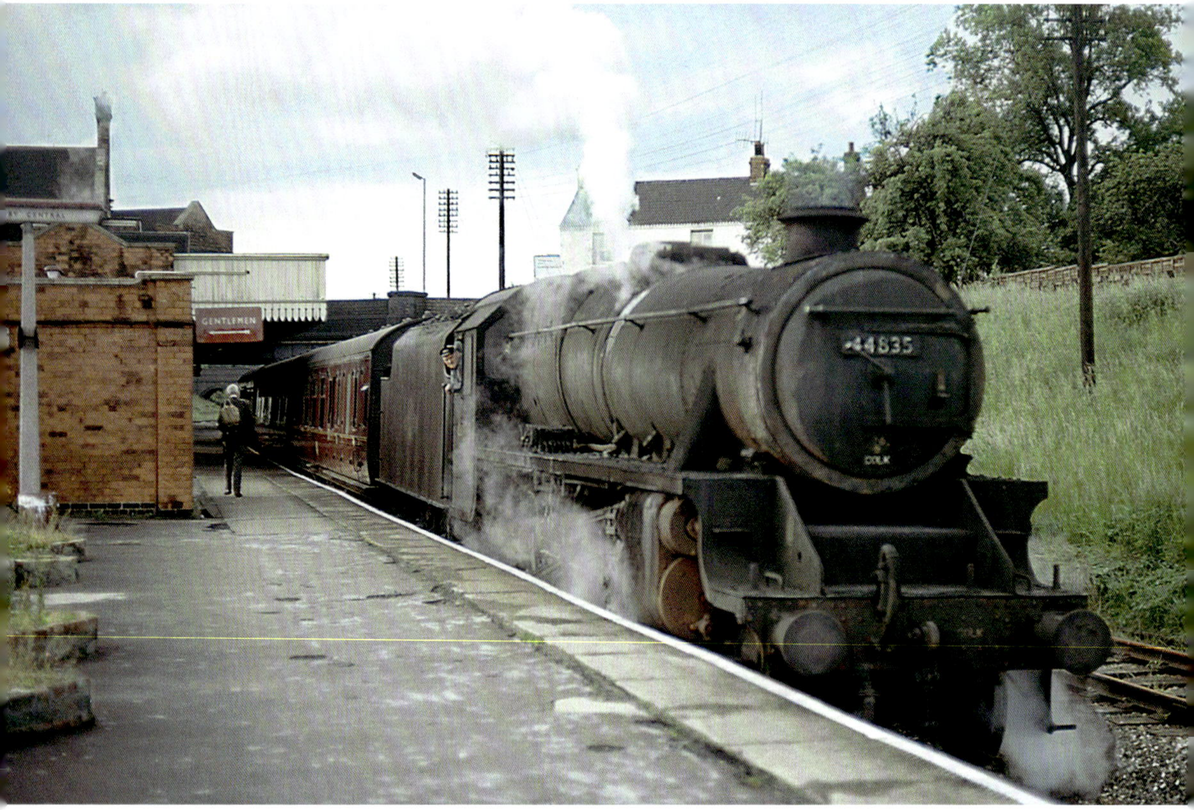
GENTLEMEN
44835

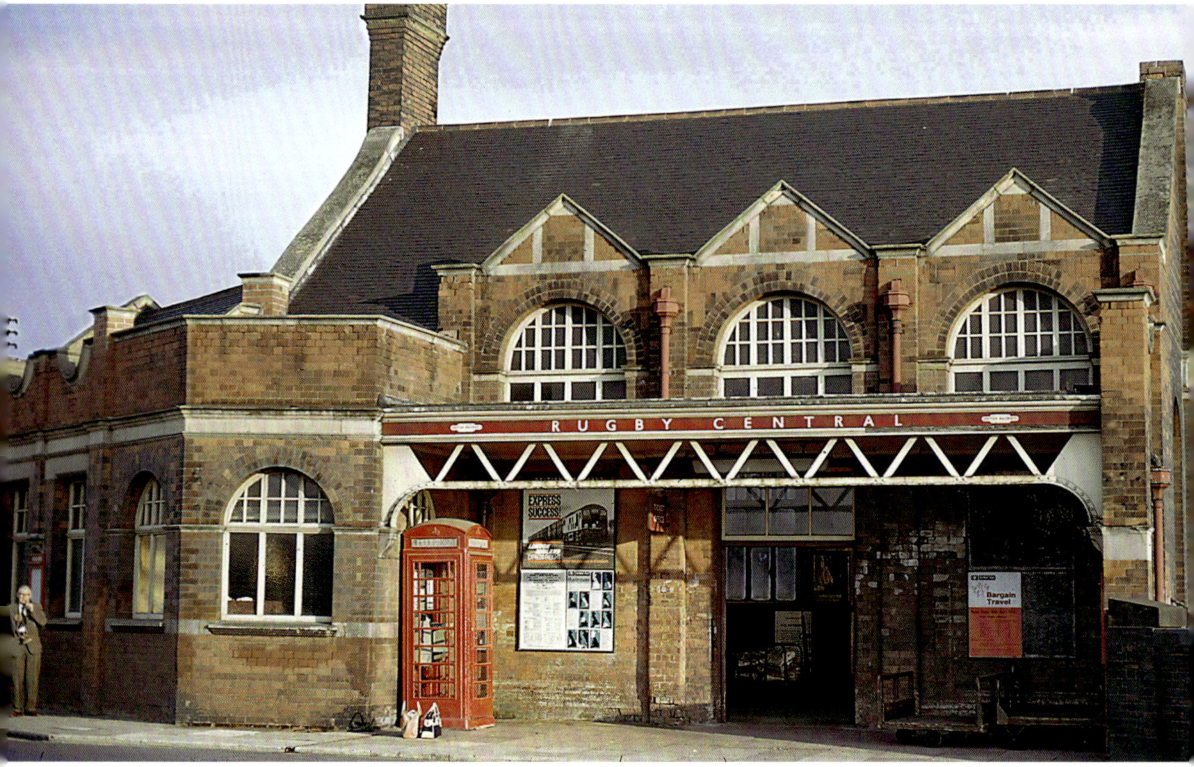
RUGBY CENTRAL
EXPRESS SUCCESS
Bargain Travel

Above, below, and opposite page: My father and Eric Parker drove to Rugby Central on 16 June 1966, where they caught the Poole/Bournemouth to York through train as far as Nottingham Victoria, hauled by Brush 'Type 4' D1873 with thirteen coaches, using this ticket. Although the local services were withdrawn in March 1963 north of Aylesbury Town, a token service was retained between Rugby Central and Nottingham Victoria. It was on the early evening three-coach 'local' that they returned to Rugby behind 'Black 5' No. 44835 and this was when all three photographs were taken—'station deserted', according to Eric Parker's diaries. Rugby Central station was situated along Hillmorton Road, some distance east of the town centre. It was another island platform station of the type preferred by the GCR, with a length of about 600 feet. On one side of Hillmorton Road were the booking hall and office plus the parcel's office, and access to platform level was down a covered staircase. Outside in the sunshine Eric Parker is having a smoke with pipe-in hand, while one of the station notices relates to the impending withdrawal of services. On the platform were three waiting rooms and a Gentlemen's urinals, the latter being the only building not covered by the canopy. Following its arrival from Nottingham, No. 44835 ran back with the empty stock (page 15) to Leicester Central, and from there it would take over the 1.15 a.m. to Nottingham Victoria the next morning. Although the line south of Rugby closed entirely to Calvert Junction on and from 5 September 1966, a local passenger service was retained north to Nottingham; this carried on until it too was withdrawn in May 1969. The station buildings were demolished after closure, although the platform still exists. Rugby Borough Council purchased the former trackbed and it is now a nature walk called the Great Central Way.

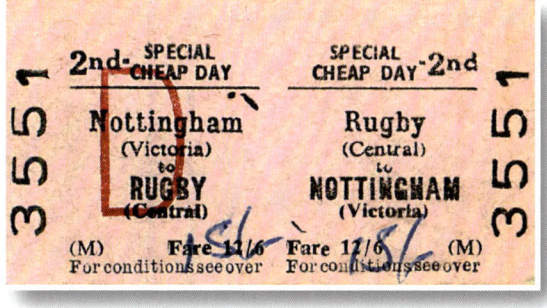

There was an over six-miles-long uphill grade of 1 in 176 on the northern approach to Charwelton that passed through Catesby Tunnel. These photographs are taken about halfway up by Staverton Road signal box, where the GCR passed over the A425 Leamington Spa to Daventry road. It is the late afternoon of Friday, 8 May 1964 and coming downhill is York-allocated V2 No. 60895, while heading towards Woodford Halse is 9F No. 92092 of Annesley shed. Note the different lamp headcodes—an express freight with the automatic brake operative on no less than half of the vehicles for the V2 (possibly the afternoon Woodford Halse to York (Dringhouses) merchandise service), while the 9F's indicates a through freight train with no automatic brake. An 'out and home' scheme for freight trains between Annesley and Woodford Halse had been introduced by the LNER in June 1947 using 2-8-0s, which was calculated to save over fifty sets of men and double the train miles per hour. The 9Fs started taking over in 1957 allowing an increase in maximum loads southbound from forty-five to fifty-five loaded mineral wagons plus better utilisation. Two return trips were possible with a third underway within twenty-four hours. It promised annual mileages of about 70,000, but the highest seems to have been 44,890 with No. 92072 in 1959 (equivalent to 340 round trips).

The first railway at Rugby was the London and Birmingham, which in turn became part of the LNWR; it was sixty years later before the GCR arrived in 1898. Heading north from Rugby Central, the GCR crossed the LNWR tracks at a right angle on a girder viaduct called the 'Birdcage Bridge'. A consequence for the LNWR was that it created sighting problems for their signalling and they built the 'Rugby Bedstead' signalling gantry, which represented the ultimate in co-acting signals: the LNWR claimed it was the largest in the UK. This photograph was taken in May/June 1966 and shows the view across to the old LNWR station from a Nottingham Victoria-bound train; between 1949 and 1969, this station was called Rugby Midland. The BR Locomotive Testing Station on the immediate left was built as a joint venture between the LMS and LNER, something Sir Nigel Gresley had campaigned long and hard for. A previous proposal intended to serve the railways and private manufacturers fell by the wayside, but work resumed after the Second World War and it was completed in 1948, with the last steam locomotive tests taking place in 1959. The large structure behind the Testing Station is Rugby engine shed's mechanical coaling plant. This reinforced concrete structure was built by the LMS and had two 150-ton-capacity coal bunkers. The original LNWR coaling stage, dating from 1876 with a water tank above it, is in the middle distance in front of the station (Rugby engine shed had closed to steam from 24 May 1965). In front of the old coaling stage are four Metropolitan Railway Bo-Bo electric locomotives dating from the 1920s; according to *The Railway Observer* of July 1965, Nos 2, 7, 16, and 18 had been stored here since March for removal of electrical fittings.

Lutterworth station is seen during the bad winter of 1962–63 on 8 February 1963, which was also the day my father visited the Leicester West Bridge branch in the snow (page 76). Initially, when the GCR's passenger service had been downgraded to semi-fast status, it was be worked by 'Cross Country'-type DMUs with refreshment facilities. Although advertised by BR, this was never provided, the official reason being a lack of refuelling facilities at Nottingham Victoria, which would have been uneconomic to provide for such a limited service. Nevertheless, from early 1963, the 8.38 a.m. from London and the 12.30 p.m. return from Nottingham were operated by one of the four-car suburban DMUs used on the local Marylebone services. Fuel capacity did not seem to be a problem on their 253 miles round trip; presumably, it used a unit that would otherwise have stood idle at Marylebone between the morning and evening peak services. With the introduction of the winter timetable in September 1963, it became a scheduled DMU working on an accelerated timing. A typical steam-hauled timing from Marylebone to Nottingham Victoria was three hours seventeen minutes, but the DMU was scheduled in two hours and forty-nine minutes, a significant saving. It included a sprint from Aylesbury to Brackley—twenty-two minutes for the 21.5 miles—and even faster on the return. The ticket is also dated 8 February 1963.

With the rise of the motor car in the 1950s, combined with falling passenger numbers on the railways, an obvious area to consider for economies was where duplicated routes existed. A famous example was Birmingham to London, which was served by both the GWR and LMS routes; another was Exeter, where both the GWR and SR had lines to London. With the GCR arriving so late on in the nineteenth century, virtually all the towns it served already had existing railways, but an exception was here at Lutterworth, a market town between Rugby and Leicester. Lutterworth's nearest pre-GCR railhead was at Ullesthorpe on the MR Rugby to Leicester line, some 4 miles away. The station layout was typical GCR with an island platform, and accessed from beneath a bridge over a bridleway at the end of Station Road, from where steps led up to the booking office at the south end of the platform. The date of both the photograph and the ticket is Thursday, 18 August 1966, the last time your author travelled on the GCR before closure at the beginning of September. With so few services over the route at the end, it was difficult to make return journeys in a short space of time, but on this occasion, my father excelled. After working until mid-afternoon, we drove to Lutterworth and caught the evening three-coach local behind No. 45222 to East Leake, where, after only a five-minute wait, we came back on another local to Lutterworth. Here, No. 44811 is seen with its three coaches about to depart on the final leg of its journey to Rugby Central.

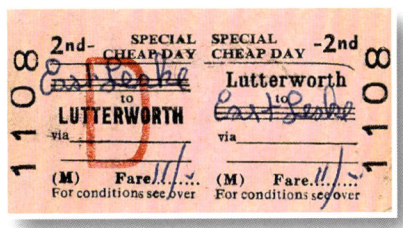

129

Ashby Magna survived the mass closure of the more rural stations along the GCR north of Aylesbury in March 1963; it was situated midway between the villages of Dunton Bassett and Ashby Magna. Both photographs were taken on the evening of 11 August 1966. The recently opened M1 was immediately to the east of the railway, the two running very close for some miles from south of Lutterworth to the approaches of Leicester. We had taken cine-film of the 5.20 p.m. local from Rugby Central from our car on the M1 and pulled onto the hard shoulder by the side of Ashby Magna station when the train stopped. Your author recalls his father getting out of the car, lifting up the bonnet, and scratching his head—hopefully, any traffic police would have thought

there was a problem with the car and not that we were waiting for the train to depart. We returned to Ashby Magna station and witnessed three passenger trains calling during the next hour. First, at 6.10 p.m., was the train in the photograph, 'Black 5' No. 44811 on the 5.15 from Nottingham Victoria to Marylebone and loaded to seven coaches (the actual departure of No. 44811 can heard in the Sound Bites section of the author's website). The signal box was still open at Ashby Magna and controlling the co-acting starter signal, thus enabling it to be seen both from a distance over the top of the road bridge and also close to when stopped at the station. At 7 p.m., No. 44984 called northbound with four coaches on the 4.38 p.m. from Marylebone, while at 7.11 p.m., No. 44847 was hauling the three-coach 6.15 p.m. Nottingham Victoria to Rugby Central. The light must have been poor for mid-August, as Eric Parker states he used 1/25 second at f 2.8, he also says 'This station rather derelict—two women porters in turn meet the arrival of the trains' (it became unstaffed from the September).

The GCR crossed much of Leicester on a viaduct that was about 1.5 miles long and involved the compulsory purchase of about 300 houses. It was on this viaduct section that Leicester Central station itself was built, a large 1,245-foot long 'H'-shaped island platform with running lines to either side and bays at both ends for local workings. This is another photograph taken on 16 June 1966 and shows 'Black 5' No. 44941 on the evening three-coach local working from Rugby Central to Nottingham Victoria. The tickets are a bit of a puzzle, as the first is dated 13 June 1966 and the second 14 June 1966, but at least it gives an indication of the number of tickets issued at this time. It might appear there was not that much variety in the type of locomotives used, or even that many trains running over the GCR London Extension in the last year or so, and while that may have some truth during the day, it was not at times during the night at Leicester. *The Railway Observer* reported just what an interesting period it was between 10.30–11 p.m. at Leicester Central during July 1966, with 'Hymek' diesel-hydraulics, Brush Type 4 diesel-electrics, and 'Black 5s'.

Above, below, and opposite page: The rundown and closure of much of the GCR's London Extension extended over about ten years or so. Probably the first sign of change to come was on 1 February 1958, when the long-rumoured inter-regional transfer took place of the GC main line from the Eastern Region of BR to the London Midland Region. As a result, from London Marylebone to south of Heath, near Chesterfield, came under LMR control, excepting around London where tracks were shared with London Transport. The long-distance express passenger services ceased at the beginning of 1960, and many of the more rural stations closed in early March 1963, replaced by the semi-fasts in conjunction with certain other services. The long-distance heavy freight traffic did last a bit longer, but by mid-1965, this had been transferred away to other routes. September 1966 saw closure of the GC's London Extension, but not its total closure. In particular, a passenger service was kept on from Nottingham Victoria to Rugby Central and operated by DMUs, although from 4 September 1967, this worked from a re-opened Arkwright Street, Nottingham (one of the stations closed in March 1963) and carried on until May 1969, when it too was withdrawn (although a freight service still continues over part of the route as well as two heritage railways). It was during this period that Leicester Central station achieved a very dubious claim to fame: becoming the largest unstaffed halt on the entire BR network. These three photographs at Leicester Central station are: the south end (colour), the north end (monochrome), plus also a train service poster from this final period. All were taken when we called in our way to a railway film show organised by Ian Allan and the National Film Theatre in Nottingham on 22 January 1967.

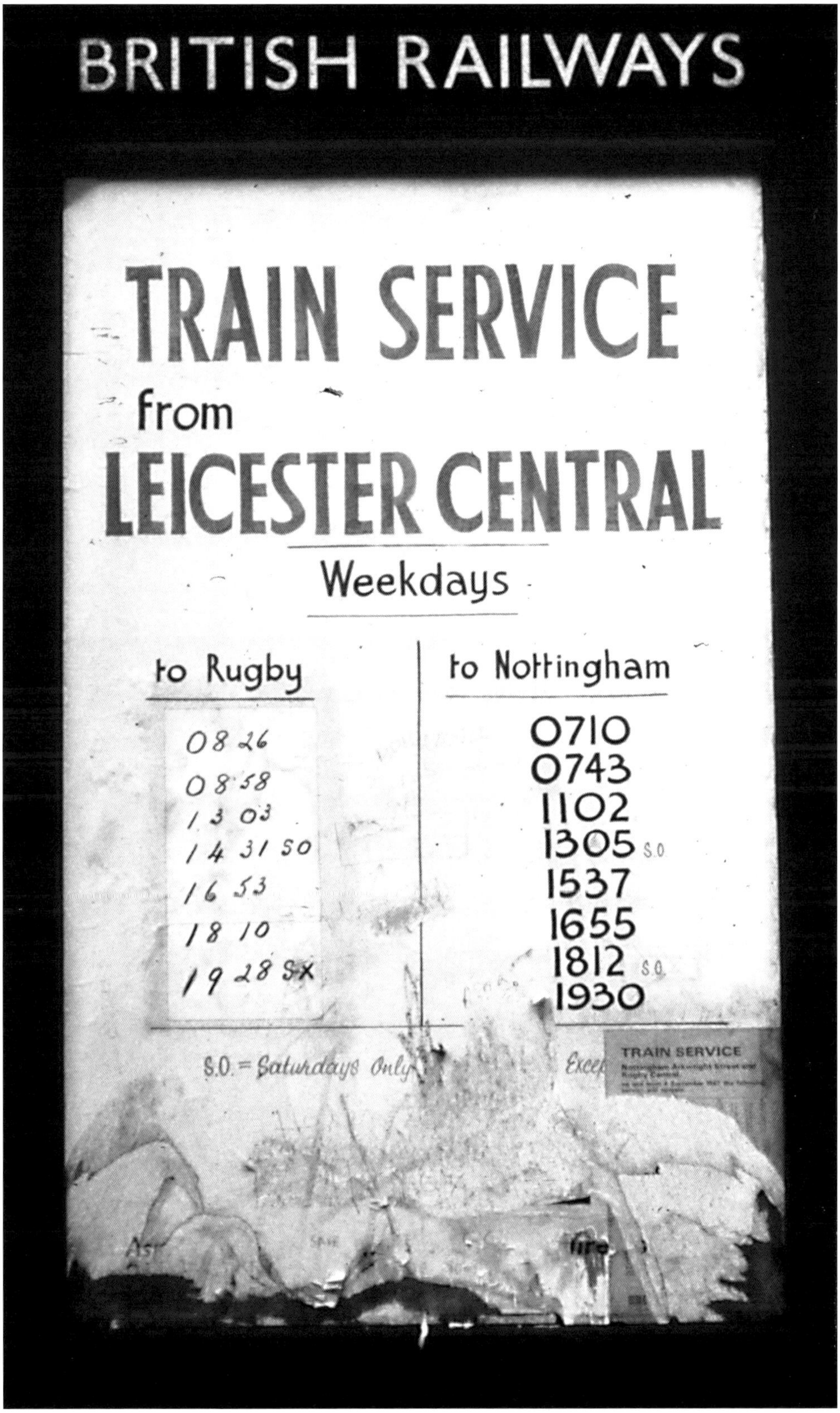

BRITISH RAILWAYS

TRAIN SERVICE from LEICESTER CENTRAL

Weekdays

to Rugby	to Nottingham
0826	0710
0858	0743
1303	1102
1431 SO	1305 SO
1653	1537
1810	1655
1928 SX	1812 SO
	1930

S.O. = Saturdays Only

Just to the north of Loughborough Central station, on the west side of the tracks, a good view could be had of the home of the Brush 'Type 4' Co-Co diesel-electric locomotives. The company had its origins in the mid-Victorian period and, in addition to locomotives and rolling stock, also built trams and trolleybuses, even diversifying to aircraft during the Second World War. One 0-4-0 tank engine built here by the Falcon Engine & Car Works Ltd in 1888 (W/N 165) has intrigued your author for many years. It came as a great surprise when an article appeared over forty years ago stating Brunel's broad-gauge was alive and well on the Azores (Portuguese islands in the Atlantic Ocean), and where this broad-gauge product of Loughborough apparently still exists today. In 1957, the works were purchased by Hawker Siddeley, and in the era of this photograph (May or June 1966) it was known as the Brush Electrical Engineering Company Limited. The works were home to what became BR's 'Standard Type 4' diesel locomotive, and eventually 512 were built from 1962 onwards; not all were built at Loughborough, with 202 being constructed at Crewe. It is difficult to read the numbers, but they appear to be D1941 through to D1945, all being added to BR's books during the early summer of 1966. For many though, I suspect that the variety of cars in the foreground may be of equal if not greater interest.

The LMS main line diesel-electric programme consisted of two Co-Co locomotives of 1,600 hp plus a single Bo-Bo of 827 hp for secondary services. The Bo-Bo was built by North British but not completed until 1950, and after trials in Scotland was handed over to the LMR receiving the number 10800. It remained in active service until 1959, when the diesel locomotives ordered under the 'Modernisation Plan' were entering service in ever increasing numbers. It was saved from scrapping by becoming a research locomotive in a joint venture between BR and Brush to examine the possibilities of squirrel-cage induction motors (AC) for rail traction purposes rather than DC. The original Paxman engine was replaced by a Bristol-Siddeley Maybach MD655 (as in the 'Westerns' and the Brush-built *Falcon*). Following the Brush tradition of bird themes, 10800 was given the name *Hawk*. In this view, thought to be taken near Loughborough during May–June 1966, it is still carrying the 10800 number and below it says 'Research Locomotive'. It undertook trial running on the GCR and was recorded by *The Railway Observer* during January 1966 on the Gotham branch and between East Leake and Loughborough Central. It appears the electronics necessary had not advanced sufficiently to make this pilot scheme a success; the finance required dried up and 10800 was scrapped in the 1970s. It took some years, but nowadays, the AC technology concerned has matured, and things like variable frequency inverters are readily available for today's railways.

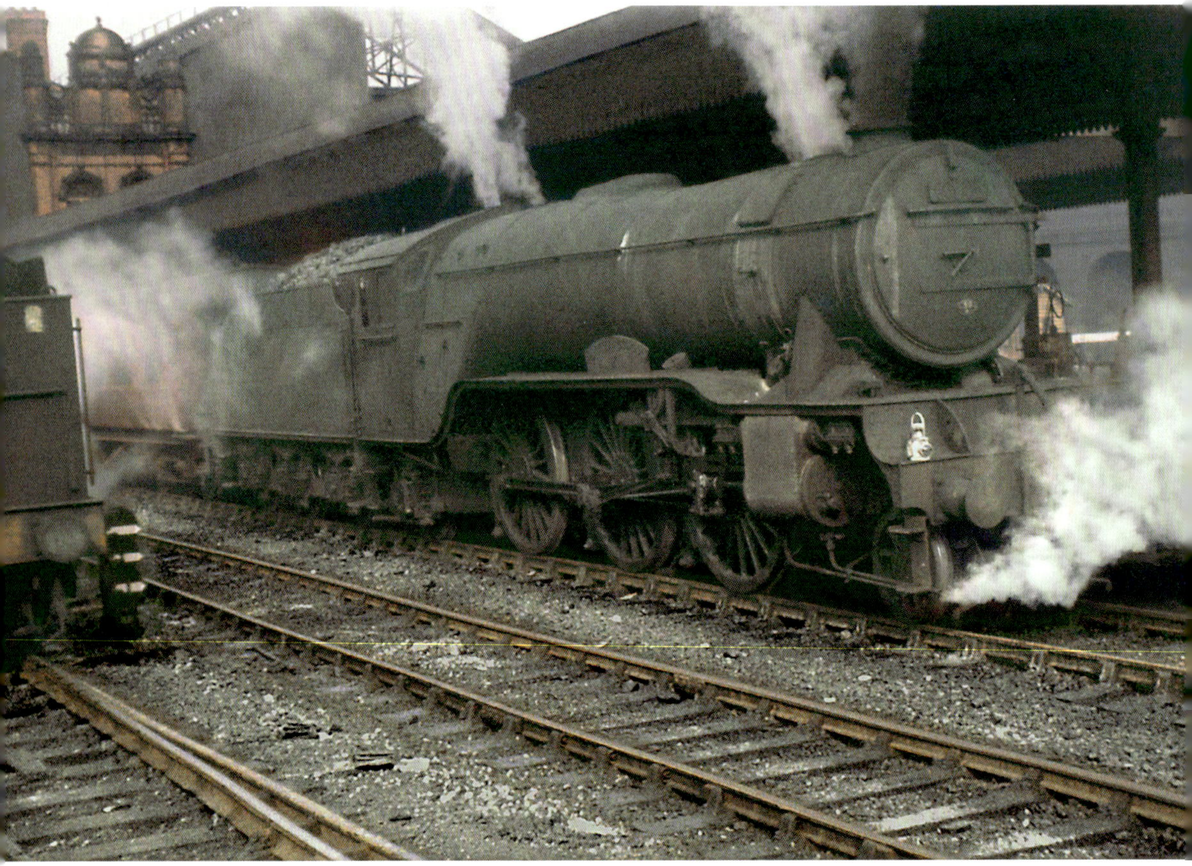

(No. 1)
2nd- SPECIAL CHEAP DAY
0953
CHILD
Chesterfield (Central) to NOTTINGHAM (Victoria)
(M) Fare 2/8
For conditions see over
(No. 1)
SPECIAL CHEAP DAY -2nd
Nottingham (Victoria) to CHESTERFIELD (Central)
(M) Fare 2/8
For conditions see over
CHILD
0953

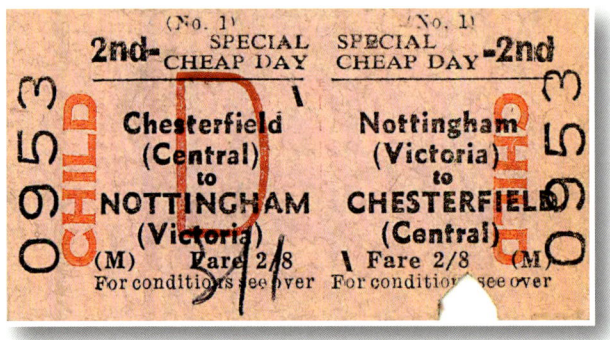

Above and opposite page: Two weeks before the withdrawal of the Sunday daytime passenger services over the GCR's London Extension, we travelled from Brackley Central to Chesterfield Central and back with a break at Nottingham Victoria. The date was Sunday, 17 February 1963 and my child's cheap day return ticket is included (from Brackley to Nottingham we travelled with ordinary returns (page 115) at a significantly higher cost per mile). Although our train from Brackley was hauled by 'Black 5' No. 45335, the Eastern Region presence was still strong at Nottingham Victoria; not long after our arrival one of the named V2s, York-allocated No. 60847 *St Peter's School York A.D. 627* departed for the south. The station pilot on this rather hazy day was B1 No. 61141 and locally based at Colwick shed, it is detaching GWR 'Siphon G' No. W2937W. The strange name came from the GWR Telegraphic Code for a milk wagon, and the first 'Siphons' appeared in the 1870s. This is a gangwayed 'G' variant, of which 175 were built between 1936 and 1955; they were derived from a strengthened classic passenger carriage. W2937W (its BR designation) was built during the Second World War and initially used for conveying churned milk. Many saw other uses subsequently: some were modified as newspaper vans when they were also fitted with steam heating.

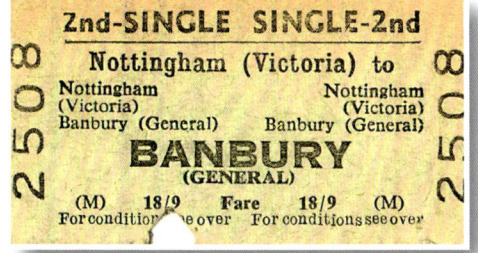 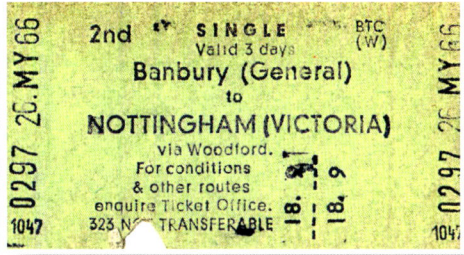

Above and opposite page: Two visits were made to Nottingham Victoria in 1966 and these photographs were both taken on the first—26 May 1966. My father travelled from Banbury to Nottingham on the Bournemouth to York through service, which, since September 1965, had actually started from Poole (although the coach destination boards still said Bournemouth–Oxford–York). He returned on the 5.15 p.m. Nottingham to Marylebone service as far as Woodford Halse. There used to be a local service between Woodford Halse and Banbury, but with the closure of Woodford Halse shed in 1965, it was provided instead by an express bus between the two, and advertised this way in the public timetable. Nottingham Victoria station could seem rather desolate latterly, with so few passenger trains over the GCR, and No. 45267 cuts a rather lonely figure at the south end while acting as station pilot; however, there was also still a DMU service that ran from Nottingham Victoria to Grantham. The return train to Woodford Halse is today hauled by No. 44847, waiting for custom on the east side of the station (see also page 14). A detailed article written by BR appeared in both the *Nottingham Guardian* and the February 1960 SLS house magazine, explaining reasons for the recently introduced GCR changes, the British Transport Commission being required by statute to make the railways pay. Duplication of passenger services at places like Nottingham and Leicester has been mentioned earlier, the MR and GCR routes effectively running more or less parallel for about 160 miles south from Sheffield. LMR management decided to concentrate a large proportion of the slow and heavy freight traffic from the East Midlands towards London on the GCR, this allowing a higher speed passenger service on the MR instead of having the problem of conflicting train speeds on both routes. Also, parcels traffic was buoyant, with a large proportion of the LMR's total originating in London, Leicester, Nottingham, and Manchester, all directly served by the GCR line. Routing this traffic over the GCR would avoid interference with MR passenger services and also with the passengers themselves, keeping them away from piles of parcels stacked on station platforms.

Although the intensive freight service from Annesley to Woodford Halse came to an end by mid-1965, there could still be considerable freight activity through Nottingham Victoria. *The Railway Observer* of December 1965 reported coal trains even running on Sundays, and, as a result of both the long block section from New Basford to Nottingham Victoria and congestion at the new Netherfield crossover to Colwick yard, there were queues of trains to Bulwell Common. It was not unusual for all southbound lines to be occupied at Nottingham Victoria and an example was quoted of seven trains so lined up—four freight trains (three steam-hauled and one diesel) and three passenger trains (two 'Britannia'-hauled and one DMU). When my father and Eric Parker visited Nottingham Victoria on 16 June 1966, they arrived at 4.43 p.m. on the Bournemouth to York working and returned on the 5.15 p.m. Marylebone service, yet in this short space of time saw four freight workings pass through. One of these four was hauled by Colwick-based No. 45222 and is seen at the north end of the station, where it can be appreciated just how much excavation work was required in the building of Nottingham Victoria. Of interest are No. 45222's larger than usual cabside numerals and also the height of coal stacked in its tender, which is possibly even taking the locomotive out of gauge.

To excavate the site of Nottingham Victoria station involved the removal of some 600,000 cubic yards of sandstone from a site about 650 yards long and 110 yards wide, and there was a tunnel at each end—its construction was a massive undertaking. It was joint station between the GCR and GNR, but they could not agree on a name; as we have seen, many GCR stations ended in 'Central' but this was unacceptable to the GNR. Eventually, the suggestion of 'Victoria' was made, with the opening date being Queen Victoria's birthday, and both parties agreed to this. The official opening date (without ceremony of any kind) became 24 May 1900. Over one year after the start of services on the railway, Nottingham Victoria comprised two large island platforms, each over 1,200 feet long with two bays at either end for local traffic, giving a total of twelve platform faces. It is again 16 June 1966, but today the 5.15 p.m. to London Marylebone has a special party onboard—The Oxford University Railway Society—and their OURS headboard is on the front of 'Black 5' No. 44936. Directing passengers for this train to Leicester, Rugby, and Marylebone was the platform indicator that also contained a selection of other potential destinations.

The splendour of Nottingham Victoria station can be appreciated from this quite stunning view looking to the south on 16 June 1966. For a short time around this period, in addition to colour slides (mainly Agfa CT18 by then), we used Gevaert Dia-Direct 35-mm black and white transparencies, and this film has certainly coped well with the difficult light conditions inside the station. The station clock shows 4.58 p.m., so plenty of time to be able to walk over the footbridge and catch the 5.15 p.m. to the south from platform ten. The last day of through services to London Marylebone was Saturday, 3 September 1966, when the semi-fasts were strengthened to eight coaches, but it was not the end of passenger services here. From Monday, 5 September, a DMU service started working along the GCR to Rugby Central in addition to the existing Grantham service from Nottingham Victoria. The Grantham service continued until the beginning of July 1967, when it was diverted to Nottingham Midland station and the ticket

booking office closed here at Victoria at the same time, the train guards issuing tickets on the Rugby DMUs instead. The next change came on and from 4 September 1967 when Arkwright Street station, Nottingham, re-opened (it had closed with many of the other local stations along the GCR north of Aylesbury in March 1963). Arkwright Street became terminus of the Rugby service and Nottingham Victoria closed completely for passenger services. By the spring of 1968, the remaining freight services were using two through lines on the extreme east of the station. This allowed developers of the Victoria Shopping Centre onto the site but, after 27 May 1968, even these two tracks were closed to traffic, the complete area being handed over to the builders, although it was 1972 before work was completed. Although the clock tower and Station Hotel (now the Hilton, Nottingham) still remain, Nottingham Victoria was razed to the ground and the sound of trains finally eliminated after seventy years.

Very little remains of the impressive Nottingham Victoria station, this clock tower being an exception. In this 1966 photograph, can you make out where the giant 'LNER VICTORIA STATION' sign used to be underneath the clock?